THE AD )F

Navigation
Exercises

THE **ADLARD COLES** BOOK OF

Navigation Exercises

ALISON NOICE
& JAMES STEVENS

ADLARD COLES NAUTICAL
London

Published by Adlard Coles Nautical
an imprint of A & C Black Publishers Ltd
37 Soho Square, London W1D 3QZ
www.adlardcoles.com

First published as **The RYA Book of Navigation Exercises** 1997
Second edition 2000
Reprinted 2001
This edition published as **The Adlard Coles Book of Navigation Exercises** 2003

ISBN 0-7136-6323-5

A CIP catalogue record for this book is available from the British Library.

A & C Black uses paper produced with elemental chlorine-free pulp, harvested from managed
sustainable forests

Typeset in 10/12pt Concorde by Falcon Oast Graphic Art
Printed and bound in Great Britain by Bell & Bain Ltd, Glasgow

The material in this book (ie chart extracts, tide tables etc) is to be used only for the purpose of
completing the exercises and not for navigation. Whilst every effort has been made to ensure
that the contents are as accurate as possible, neither the authors nor publishers can accept any
responsibility for errors or omissions that may be found.

Contents

Foreword

'Navigation is yesterday's problem. Today we have instant access to highly accurate electronic position fixing information, so why should anyone need to learn about navigation?'

We have indeed, for the last few years, had the ability to fix our position at sea quickly and accurately, in all conditions of visibility, by day or night. But to conclude that this means that we no longer need navigational skills would be a very dangerous mistake. Ever since affordable electronic position fixing has been a feature of yacht navigation, the annual figures for Lifeboat launches to stranded yachts have shown a steady year-on-year increase.

Position fixing has never been more than a part of the navigator's problem. In the distant past, before we had accurate clocks, it posed enormous problems to the ocean voyager. Over the years we have solved these problems so that today the more significant navigational question is not 'Where am I?' but 'Where do we go from here?'

Now that we have such high levels of potential accuracy it is possible to navigate with much tighter safety margins, and this places ever higher demands on navigational skills. This book makes a significant contribution to those skills, at two important levels.

For the beginner who is learning navigation, the ability to test newly-acquired skills is probably the most important part of the learning process. For the more experienced navigator, opportunities to practise every aspect of his or her art will inevitably be limited, so a set of exercises is invaluable for keeping in practice.

There can be few people with better credentials to produce this book than Alison Noice and James Stevens. They have both been involved with teaching navigation, at all levels, for many years, so they know exactly which of the subject areas cause difficulty in the classroom. Even more importantly, they are both active and practical yacht navigators, and their work is not just about academic exercises, it carries the essential authority of the practical exponent of the navigator's art.

Bill Anderson
Training Manager
Royal Yachting Association

Introduction

These exercises are for all those wishing to brush up their navigation skills, including students on RYA shorebased courses. In each exercise the questions become progressively more advanced. If you can answer all of them you have most of the theory knowledge required to be a Yachtmaster or Coastal Skipper. Day Skippers should be able to answer the first part of each exercise.

A practice chart and tables are included in this book. No further charts, almanacs or pilot books are required to complete the exercises.

Equipment

You will need a plotting instrument such as a Portland or Breton plotter, and dividers which you can purchase from a chandlery shop. Also a 2B pencil and a good eraser.

Accuracy

You should aim to navigate to a precision of 0.1 mile and 1° for chartwork, and 0.1 metre for tidal calculations.

At sea it is not always necessary to navigate to this level of precision, but a good yacht skipper knows that precise navigation in, say, fog or other adverse conditions can greatly enhance the safety of the passage. Accurate navigation also allows the skipper to explore new and interesting ports and anchorages.

Finally, remember that the main reason for becoming more competent at sea is to gain more pleasure from the sport.

Alison Noice
James Stevens

Part I

NAVIGATION EXERCISES

1. Nautical Terms and Seamanship

1.1

Which letters refer to the following?

1	Liferaft	9	Lifebelt	17	Lifebelt light
2	Waterline	10	Forehatch	18	Keel
3	Jib luff	11	Stemhead	19	Forestay
4	Gooseneck	12	Pulpit	20	Guardrail
5	Reef pennant	13	Danbuoy	21	Stanchion
6	Clew	14	Reef point	22	Batten
7	Rudder	15	Winch	23	Jib sheet
8	Mainsheet	16	Propeller	24	Skeg

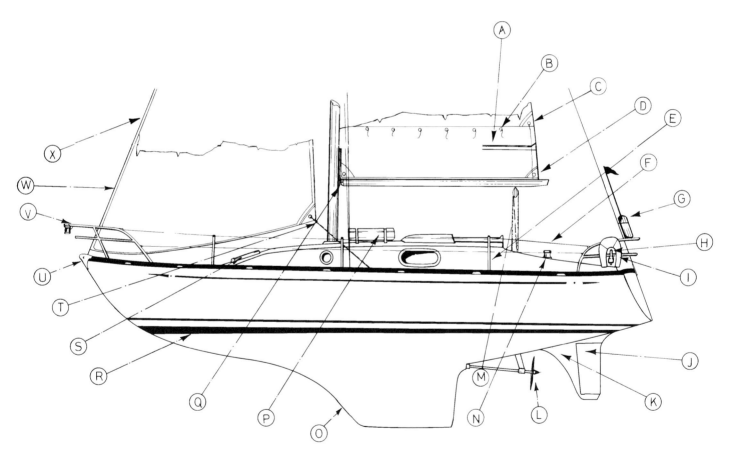

Turn to page 37 for answers

Nautical Terms and Seamanship *continued*

1.2

Which letters refer to the following?

1 Windlass	**7** Liferaft	**13** Stanchion
2 Stemhead	**8** Gunwale	**14** Bridge deck
3 Propeller	**9** Windscreen	**15** Rudder
4 Radar scanner	**10** Bathing platform	**16** Transom
5 Davit	**11** Chine	
6 Trim tab	**12** Guardrail	

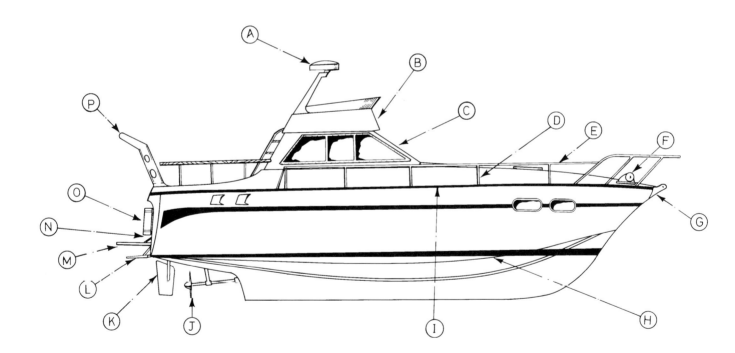

Turn to page 37 for answers

Nautical Terms and Seamanship continued

1.3

Which letters on the diagram refer to the following?

1	Chart table
2	Cockpit locker
3	Engine
4	Bulkhead
5	Heads
6	Galley
7	Companionway steps
8	Quarter berth
9	Saloon berth
10	Forepeak berth
11	Saloon table
12	Chain locker
13	Gas locker

Which numbers on the diagram refer to the following?

A	To windward
B	Astern
C	Starboard beam
D	Port quarter
E	Starboard quarter
F	Starboard bow
G	Port beam

wind ➡

Turn to page 37 for answers

7

Nautical Terms and Seamanship *continued*

1.4

What are the names and uses of the following knots and hitches?

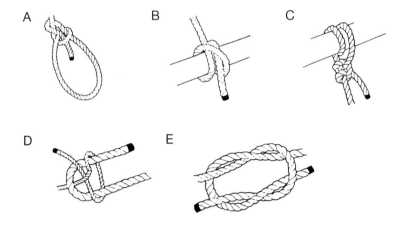

A B C

D E

1.5

What are the following points of sail?

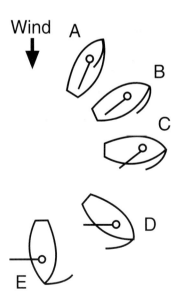

Wind A

B

C

D

E

Turn to page 37 for answers

Nautical Terms and Seamanship continued

1.6

Draw the ropes you would use to secure the yacht against the quay. It is half tide. The range of the tide is 3 metres.

1.7

Match the controls to the effect on a power boat.

A	Starboard trim down	**1**	Bow up
B	Port trim down	**2**	Bow down
C	Outdrive aft	**3**	Correct list to port
D	Starboard trim up	**4**	Correct list to starboard
E	Port trim up		
F	Outdrive forward		

Turn to page 38 for answers

2. Chart Familiarisation

Use chart RYA 1.

2.1

On Admiralty charts from which level

   a) are depths measured on the chart?
   b) are heights measured on the chart?

2.2

What indication is given that the UK Hydrographic Office publish a larger scale chart of Plymouth Sound? What is the chart number?

2.3

On chart RYA 1 what is the significance of:

   a) the magenta tinted area between the island of Alderney and Lizard Point? (Top half of chart, left-hand side.)
   b) the green tinted area close to the shore?
   c) the purple 'tear-drop' next to some navigational buoys?
   d) the pale blue shading at sea?

2.4

What are the meanings of the following symbols?

a)   b)   c)   d) ~~~ e) FS

f)  g)   h)   i)   j) —3kn→

2.5

What is the nature of the bottom in the following positions? (Top half of chart)

   a) 090°(T) from the eastern side of Looe Island   3.8M
   b) 170°(T) from Plymouth Breakwater Lighthouse   3.5M
   c) 120°(T) from Dodman Point Monument   7.1M

Turn to page 39 for answers

Chart Familiarisation continued

2.6

What are the meanings of the symbols at the following positions? (Bottom half of chart)

a) 49° 25'.6N   04° 59'.8W
b) 49° 31'.8N   05° 01'.9W
c) 49° 26'.6N   06° 05'.0W
d) 49° 05'.9N   06° 04'.3W

2.7

Using the bottom half of the chart, measure the following **true** bearings and distances from:

a) St Martin's Point Lighthouse (south-east corner of Guernsey) to L'Etac, a small island on the south-east corner of Sark?
b) Flamanville church (49° 38'.2N   05° 01'.7W) to Platte Fougère Lighthouse on the north-east corner of Guernsey?
c) Dahouet GW beacon tower (49° 04'.0N   05° 47'.8W) to Rohein YBY Light Beacon (offshore in Baie de Saint-Brieuc)?
d) Point Corbière Lighthouse (south-west corner of Jersey) to Le Grand Jardin Lighthouse (entrance channel to St Malo)?

2.8

The following is an extract from Notices to Mariners. Make these corrections on chart RYA 1.

INDEX OF CHARTS AFFECTED
Admiralty Chart Number   *Notices*
RYA Training chart 1   9843, 9844

9843 England – South Coast – West Channel – Wreck
Delete wreck symbol in position 50° 08'.7N   05° 30'.0W
Chart (last correction) RYA Training chart 1 9842/98

9844 England – South Coast – West Channel – Dodman Point Southwards – Buoy
Move special mark FLY 10s from   50° 08'.5N   05°41'.6W
                            to   50° 09'.2N   05°42'.0W
Chart (last correction) RYA Training chart 1 9843/98

Turn to page 39 for answers

11

3. Compass

Use chart RYA 1.

3.1

What is the magnetic variation at 49° 25'.0N 05° 55'.0W in the year 2000?

3.2

Convert the **magnetic** bearings to **true**.

    a) 093° (M) Variation 8°W
    b) 187° (M) Variation 6°E
    c) 002° (M) Variation 1°E
    d) 357° (M) Variation 3°W

3.3

Convert these **true** bearings to **magnetic**.

    a) 256° (T) Variation 4°W
    b) 009° (T) Variation 3°E
    c) 355° (T) Variation 8°W
    d) 002° (T) Variation 7°E

3.4

What is compass deviation?

3.5

A skipper notices that the deviation on a yacht's steering compass is greater when the yacht is sailing to windward in strong winds than in calm weather. What might cause this?

Turn to page 40 for answers

Compass *continued*

3.6

Complete the table below.

True	Variation	Magnetic	Deviation	Compass
231°		237°		239°
079°	3°E			076°
	4°W	151°		150°
	2°E	011°	2°W	
348°	2°W		1°E	

3.7

A helmsman heading towards Sark from the west is steering to keep the monument and the radio aerial in transit. The steering compass reads 072°(C).

   a) What is the true bearing of this transit?
   b) What is the magnetic bearing with a variation of 7°W?
   c) What is the deviation on this heading?

Turn to page 40 for answers

4. Position Fixing

Variation 7°W

4.1

Plot these GPS positions on the top half of chart RYA 1.

a) Waypoint: East Channel light buoy (eastern end of Separation Scheme) 310°(T) 6.1M (bearing towards waypoint)

b) Waypoint: 50° 10'.0N 05° 20'.0W 140°(T) 4.0M

4.2

Plot the following positions:

a) Monument at entrance to River Erme   047°(M)
    Coastguard lookout near Stoke Point   327°(M)
    Left hand side of Burgh Island   075°(M)

b) Windmotor near Yealm Head   074°(M)
    Church tower west of Yealm entrance   031°(M)
    LHS Great Mew Stone   349°(M)

c) Penlee Point in transit with Plymouth breakwater light   056°(M)
    Rame Head in transit with monument   349°(M)
    Depth 42m, height of tide 4m.

    Comment on the accuracy of this fix.

d) House eastern side Fowey entrance   040°(M)
    Daymark on Gribbin Head   356°(M)
    Radio tower at 50° 16'.0N 05° 42'.7W   266°(M)

    How could the navigator quickly confirm whether his position lies at the northern or southern end of the cocked hat?

e) Radio tower between Port Wrinkle and Seaton   075°(M)
    East Looe breakwater light   269°(M)
    Depth (reduced to soundings)   7m

    Comment on the accuracy of this fix.

4.3

A motor cruiser is on passage from Plymouth to Guernsey in early February. It is MHWS. At 1830 the navigator raises Casquets light and Gros du Raz light at Cap de la Hague simultaneously. The height of eye is 2m. What is the cruiser's approximate position?

Use Lights table on page 76.

4.4

At 1600 a yacht leaves St Malo on passage to Falmouth in moderate to poor visibility. An electrical fault has caused a failure of all the navigation instruments including the log. At 0200 a horn, 1 blast every 20 seconds, is heard on a bearing of about 085°(M). A ship is seen on a SW course. Previously all ships have been travelling NE. Give an approximate position.

Turn to page 41 for answers

5. International Regulations for Preventing Collisions at Sea

5.1

a)   To which side do you keep in a narrow channel?

b)   What do the rules state about sailing vessels and vessels under 20m in narrow channels?

5.2

a)   How can you establish whether a risk of collision exists when in sight of an approaching vessel?

b)   At night how can you ensure that your avoiding action is immediately obvious to the other vessel?

5.3

In the following situations a risk of collision exists. Which is the give-way vessel and what action should she take?

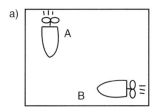
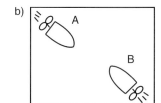
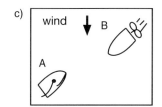

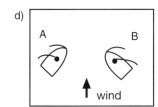
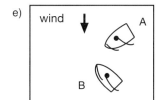
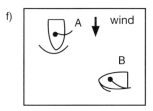

5.4

When crossing a Traffic Separation Scheme should your heading or ground track be at right angles to the traffic flow?

5.5

What sound signals are made in reduced visibility by the following craft?

a)   A yacht under sail.

b)   A vessel trawling.

c)   A power-driven vessel underway but stopped.

d)   A pilot vessel underway on duty.

e)   A yacht motorsailing.

f)   A 40m vessel at anchor.

g)   A vessel restricted in its ability to manoeuvre.

h)   A single towed vessel.

Turn to page 42 for answers

International Regulations for Preventing Collisions at Sea *continued*

5.6

What type of vessel is indicated by each of the following groups of lights? Give its probable length and aspect and whether it is underway, making way, or stopped.

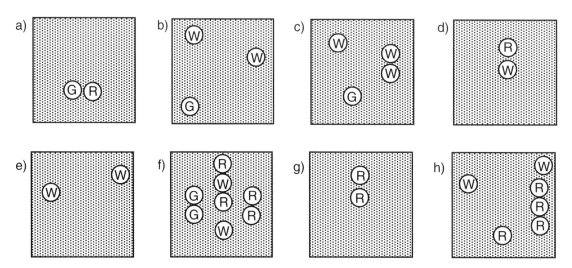

5.7

At dusk, in decreasing visibility, a yacht skipper motorsailing switches on the tricolour, steaming light and pulpit bicolour to make the yacht as visible as possible. Is this permitted in the rules?

5.8

What are the meanings of the following day shapes?

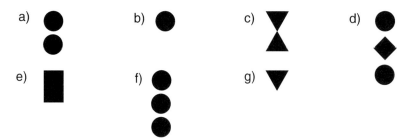

5.9

List four situations when a sailing vessel, close hauled on starboard tack, would be the give-way vessel.

Turn to page 43 for answers

6. Safety

6.1

You are skipper of the yacht *Alpha* on passage to Salcombe from the east. There are three crew on board and yourself as skipper. At 0100 hrs in heavy seas, the yacht strikes a submerged object and starts to sink. Start Point is 3 miles to the north. You decide to abandon to the liferaft. Write down the VHF message you would send.

6.2

What type of fire extinguisher would you position:

  a) Near the exits?
  b) Near the galley?
  c) In the engine space?

6.3

A rescue helicopter is overhead preparing to lift off an injured crewman. A weighted line is lowered on to the yacht. What action should the yacht crew take?

6.4

When would you direct your crew to wear:

  a) Lifejackets?
  b) Safety harnesses?
  c) What parts of the yacht are suitable for securing safety harnesses?

6.5

What type of pyrotechnic should you use when:

  a) A Search and Rescue aircraft is looking for you by day?
  b) You can see the lights of a lifeboat looking for you at night but are unsure whether the coxswain has seen you?
  c) To illuminate a man overboard at night?

6.6

List six actions to be taken as fog approaches.

Turn to page 44 for answers

7. Tidal Heights

Use chart RYA 1.

Time zones vary from question to question, so read the question carefully!

7.1

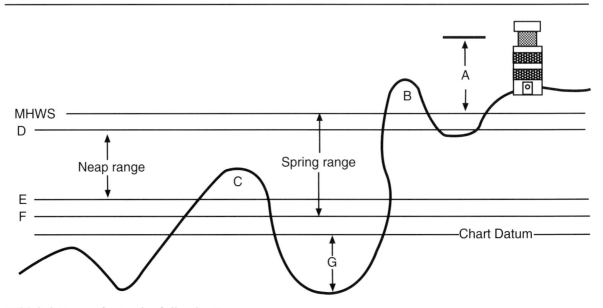

Which letters refer to the following?

1) Rock which covers and uncovers
2) Rock which does not cover
3) Charted height
4) Charted depth

5) MHWN
6) MLWS
7) MLWN

7.2

Using the tide level table at the top right-hand corner of chart RYA 1:

a) What would be the depth over Lath Rock 50° 12'.5N   05° 47'.2W at MHWN? Use Falmouth data.

b) What would be the depth at 49° 47'.4N   05° 06'.8W at MLWS? Use Goury data.

c) What would be the depth of the shallowest part of the entrance channel to the marina at Dahouet at MHWS? Use chartlet of Dahouet (on page 80) for data.

d) Would the rock at 49° 49'.8N   05° 19'.3W on the inset chart of Alderney Harbour be visible above the surface at MLWN?

e) Could a yacht with a draught of 1.2m pass over the shallowest part of Fresnaye Bay (10 miles west of St Malo) at MHWN with a clearance of 0.3m? Use data for St Malo.

f) A navigator on board a 2m draught yacht, with a mast height of 16m, wishes to take it up the River Fal and under a telephone cable charted as having a clearance of 14m. The charted depth near the cable is drying 1.0m and it is springs. Is there any state of the tide when this is possible?

7.3

At approximately what times (UT) do High Water Springs occur at Plymouth?

Turn to page 45 for answers

Tidal Heights continued

7.4

Give the times and heights of high and low water at Plymouth on the following days:
(Remember to use the time zone appropriate to the date.)

a) Before noon on Tuesday 23 January.
b) After noon on Sunday 28 April.
c) Before noon on Thursday 4 April.

7.5

What will be the range of the tide on the following days? Is it neaps, springs or halfway?

a) Before noon on Wednesday 31 January at Plymouth?
b) After noon on Monday 3 June at St Malo?
c) Before noon on Tuesday 23 April at Plymouth?

7.6

A bilge-keeled yacht, draught 1.2m, is moored in Plymouth where the charted drying height is
2.0m during the afternoon of Friday 5 April. At what time BST will she float?

7.7

At 1657 UT on Friday 29 March a yacht with a draught of 1.5m is at anchor in Plymouth in 2.7m
of water. What will be the clearance, if any, at low water?

7.8

What are the times and heights of high and low water on Thursday 18 April at Par? (See entry for
Fowey.) Give your answer in BST.

7.9

At 1611 (French Summer Time) on Sunday 21 July a yacht grounds at the entrance to Diélette.
At what time will she float again? What will be the height of tide at that time? Use corrections
for Flamanville.

7.10

A yacht skipper wishes to anchor off Mevagissey at 2242 UT on Saturday 23 March. If the
draught of the yacht is 1.7m, what is the minimum depth of water in which to anchor to ensure a
clearance of 1m at low water?

7.11

What effect can the following have on tidal heights?

a) High barometric pressure.
b) Low barometric pressure and storm force winds.

Turn to pages 45–46 for answers

8. Tidal Streams

Use chart RYA 1. Time zones vary from question to question.
Questions 8.4 d–g require the use of the computation of rates table on page 88.

8.1

Using tidal diamond ◇N◇ from the tidal stream table (bottom right on chart RYA 1), what is the direction and rate of the tidal stream:

    a) 5 hours before HW Plymouth, springs?
    b) 1 hour after HW Plymouth, neaps?
    c) 1 hour before HW Plymouth, midway between springs and neaps?

8.2

Use the tidal stream chartlets on pages 84 and 85. What will be the direction and rate of the tidal stream:

    a) 5 miles SSE of Salcombe 1 hour after HW Plymouth, springs?
    b) Between Alderney and France 5 hours before HW Plymouth at neaps?

You can use a Breton plotter to measure the angle of the arrows.

8.3

It is Friday 19 April and you are planning to cross from Alderney to Falmouth in your 35ft motor cruiser which cruises at 22kn. The wind is NE4. Would it be prudent to depart after an early breakfast, or delay until after lunch? Give reasons.

8.4

What is the direction and rate of the tidal stream at the following positions:

    a) Approximately 5M N of Cherbourg at 1844 UT on Saturday 20 January?
    b) South of Lizard Point at 1035 BST on Sunday 28 April?
    c) At 49° 56'.6N 05° 34'.3W at 1255 UT on Sunday 11 February?
    d) Between Alderney and France at 0330 UT on Tuesday 20 February? (Use tidal stream atlas for rate and plotter to measure the direction.)
    e) About 5½M 120°(T) from EC 'A' buoy in mid channel at 0630 UT on Monday 11 March?
    f) Approximately 6½M south of Wembury Bay at 2215 BST on Wednesday 17 April?
    g) At 49° 41'.9N 05° 30'.5W at 1500 UT on Wednesday 21 February?

Turn to page 47 for answers

Tidal Streams *continued*

8.5

Using the tidal stream chartlets:

a) At what time (French Summer Time) does the stream become west-going to the west of Cherbourg before noon on Monday 15 April?

b) At what time (French Standard Time) does the stream become north-going off Carteret after noon on Tuesday 2 January?

8.6

How might the tidal streams between Dahouet and Binic (bottom left corner of chart) differ from those further offshore at Grand Léjon light? Give reasons.

8.7

Would you use a tidal stream atlas or tidal diamonds in the following circumstances?

a) For planning a passage from Plymouth to Jersey.

b) For shaping a course to steer from Cherbourg to Salcombe.

c) For planning a departure time for a coastal passage from Plymouth to Falmouth.

Turn to page 48 for answers

EXERCISES

9. Estimated Position

Use chart RYA 1. Variation 7°W. Time zones vary from question to question.

The chart corrections in exercise 2.8 should be entered before starting this exercise.
For questions 5–7 use the computation of rates table on page 88.
For questions 6 and 7 also use the deviation table on page 87.

9.1

At 0900 a boat skipper fixes position next to NGS East spherical buoy 50° 11'.2N 04° 58'.9W.
Log reading 40.0. Plot the estimated position at 1000 when the log reads 47.0 and the course
steered has been 095° (M) with no leeway. The tidal stream for this period was 100°(T) 2kn.

9.2

Using the information in the log extract below, plot the estimated position.

Date	Time	Log	Course	Wind	Leeway	Bar	Notes
23 February	0914	4.0	200°(M)	NE2	Nil	1010	Fix next to yellow conical buoy 1.2M south of Plymouth breakwater
UT	1014	10.2	200°(M)	NE2	Nil	1010	EP using ◁C▷

9.3

Using the information in the log extract below, plot the estimated position.

Date	Time	Log	Course	Wind	Leeway	Bar	Notes
28 April	1026	61.8	020°(M)	E1	Nil	998	Position 1M due east of EC 'A' Channel buoy
BST	1226	69.5	020°(M)	E1	Nil	998	EP using ◁F▷ for 1 hour then ◁C▷

9.4

Using the information in the log extract below, plot the estimated position.

Date	Time	Log	Course	Wind	Leeway	Bar	Notes
6 April	1246	32.1	260°(M)	NW5	10°	1002	Position 1M west of EC 'B' Channel buoy
BST	1346	37.3	260°(M)	NW5	10°	1003	EP using ◁F▷

What is the true course over the ground?
What is the speed over the ground?

Turn to pages 49–52 for answers

Estimated Position *continued*

9.5

Using the information in the log extract below, plot the estimated position.

Date	Time	Log	Course	Wind	Leeway	Bar	Notes
4 March French Std. Time	1300	3.3	010°(M)	SW3	Nil	997	Position Cherbourg Western entrance
	1500	12.4	010°(M)	SW3	Nil	997	EP using ◇J

How close was the yacht to the Cherbourg Fairway buoy, shown on chart as 'CH1' L Fl. 10s?

9.6

Using the information in the log extract below, plot the estimated position.

Date	Time	Log	Course	Wind	Leeway	Bar	Notes
14 April BST	1237	18.1	152°(C)	E5	10°	1020	Position 50° 00'.0N 05° 43'.0W
	1350	23.9	152°(C)	E5	10°	1020	Alter course to 210°(C) to avoid ships. Leeway now nil.
	1400	24.9	210°(C)	E5	Nil	1019	Alter back to 152°(C) Leeway now 10°
	1437	28.1	152°(C)	E5	10°	1019	EP using ◇H

9.7

At 0748 UT on Wednesday 20 March the yacht navigator fixes position 49° 59'.0N 05° 55'.0W, log 21.8. The course is 114°(C) beating against an easterly wind making 10° leeway. Boat speed is 6kn. The skipper wishes to know when to tack to avoid the Traffic Separation Scheme.

What will the log read when the yacht reaches the edge of the TSS (outer edge of the magenta marking)? Use ◇E.

Turn to pages 53–5 for answers

23

10. Buoyage and Lights

Use chart RYA 1.

10.1

What is the direction of buoyage on chart RYA 1?

10.2

Sketch the topmarks of eight different navigational marks, the positions of which are shown in the diagram, and indicate which one should be placed in each position.

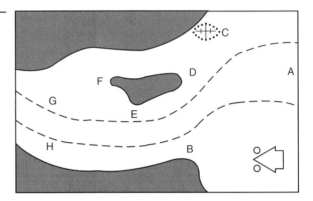

10.3

You are heading in an easterly direction when you sight a pillar buoy which is painted black at the top and yellow at the bottom. Unfortunately the topmark is missing. Do you leave the buoy on your port or starboard side?

10.4

You are sailing northwards into an estuary at night. On which side of the vessel would you leave the following lights?

a) VQ (3) 5s   c) Oc 2 G   e) Q (9) 15s   g) 2 FG (vert)
b) Fl (2) 10s   d) Iso 10s   f) Fl (2) R 6s

10.5

What would be the characteristics of Eddystone Rock Lighthouse when observed from Hand Deeps which lies approximately 3½ miles NW of Eddystone?

10.6

Quénard Point Lighthouse, on the NE corner of Alderney, is shown as having a 28M light (top left-hand corner of chart). Could it be seen from the cockpit of a small yacht at this range? Give reasons.

Turn to page 56 for answers

Buoyage and Lights *continued*

10.7

Identify the following lights which are situated on the coastline of France:

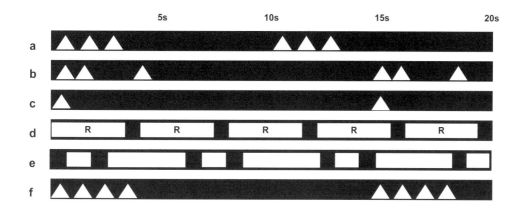

Turn to page 56 for answers

11. Course to Steer

**Use chart RYA 1. Variation 7°W. Time zones vary from question to question.
Question 11.4 uses the deviation table on page 87.
Questions 5 to 7 use the deviation table on page 87 and computation of rates table on page 88.**

11.1

At 1030 a sea angling boat is at West Trouveé buoy (approx 6M south of Jersey). Speed through the water is 6kn. Tidal stream 320°(T) 1.8kn.

    a) What is the magnetic course to steer to the VQ north cardinal mark situated approx 2M SE of Corbiére Lighthouse on Jersey?

    b) What will be the speed over the ground?

11.2

At 1530 BST a motor cruiser fixes position by GPS 49° 21'.5N 05° 34'.8W. Speed 11kn.
HW Plymouth 1900 BST Springs. Use ⟨R⟩.

    a) What will be the magnetic course to steer to the Le Vieux Banc north cardinal buoy (close NW of St Malo Fairway buoy)?

    b) What will be the speed over the ground?

    c) What will be the ETA?

11.3

At 1043 UT on Saturday 23 March, a yacht fixes position by GPS 49° 20'.0N 05° 50'.0W while on passage from Guernsey to Saint Quay-Portrieux (bottom left-hand corner of chart). Boat speed is 5kn and the craft is not making any leeway. What is the magnetic course to steer to the 17m sounding to the north of Grand Léjon lighthouse? Use ⟨Q⟩.

11.4

At 1327 BST on Thursday 25 April, a yacht is at East Trouvée east cardinal mark to the south of Jersey. Boat speed is 6kn. What is the compass course to steer to Rochefort YBY beacon tower approximately 5M to the south? Use ⟨R⟩ and the deviation table.

11.5

At 1400 French Standard Time on Wednesday 24 January, a dive support vessel is close to Madeux Beacon, just to the north of Saint-Quay-Portrieux, intending to take divers to the 20m wreck in position 49° 18'.0N 05° 58'.6W. Boat speed 10kn. What is the compass course to steer to the wreck? Use ⟨Q⟩, the deviation table and computation of rates table. *Note*: The dive will not take place until slack water.

Turn to pages 57–61 for answers

Course to Steer *continued*

11.6

A sailing yacht is at the Lower Heads buoy, south of Herm Island (east of Guernsey) at 2100 BST on Tuesday 9 April.

a) What is the compass course to steer to a waypoint in position 49° 22'.0N 05° 23'.3W if the yacht is logging 5kn with no leeway? Use ⬦N⬦ and all the relevant tables.

b) At what time (BST) will the yacht be closest to Le Chats west cardinal buoy?

c) What would be the compass course to steer to counteract 5° leeway in a SW wind?

11.7

At 1230 BST on Saturday 13 April a yacht's navigator took the following bearings in good visibility when the boat was west of Guernsey and the log read 34.6:

a) Hanois lighthouse in transit with chimney
on south-west corner of Guernsey   118°(M)
St Peter's Church tower   109°(M)
Headland north of Vale Church   080°(M)
Chimney inshore of Lihou Island in transit
with aerial in centre of island   097°(M)

Plot the fix and comment on its reliability.

b) What is the compass course to steer to a point 1M south of Hanois lighthouse if leeway is 10° in a southerly wind and the boat speed is 5kn? Use ⬦L⬦ and all relevant tables.

Turn to pages 61–3 for answers

EXERCISES

12. Navigational Instruments

12.1

Why might a GPS satellite-derived position of an object differ from the charted position?

12.2

What is:

    a) A waypoint?
    b) Cross track error?

12.3

On a 12 hour passage across the English Channel at 5kn, is it quicker to follow the rhumb line as displayed on a GPS receiver or plot a course to steer to counter the sum of the tides and be drifted off and on the rhumb line?

12.4

A crew member falls overboard at night off the island of Sark. The Man Overboard (MOB) emergency button on the GPS is activated and a course and distance is displayed back to the position where she fell in. She is not there. How would you plan your search?

12.5

You are sailing offshore when you discover that your batteries have run down to a point where you cannot start the engine to recharge them. Your navigation instruments are inoperative but the yacht is still sailing well. In order to predict your landfall you need to obtain an idea of boat speed. Is there any way you can do this without any instrumentation?

Turn to page 64 for answers

13. Pilotage

Use chart RYA 1.

13.1

Approaching harbour the leading marks are given as the circle on the rear post and the Y on the front marker. If they appear as shown which way would you alter course to bring them in transit?

13.2

The rock 'Pierre au Vraic' is situated approximately 2M off the south-west corner of Alderney and is a known danger to small craft at certain states of the tide.

If you were on passage from Alderney Harbour to Guernsey using the Swinge Channel (passage between Alderney and Burhou) in good visibility, how could you ensure that you had cleared this rock?

13.3

You are the navigator of a yacht planning to enter Plymouth at night. Use the information on pages 78–9 to write pilotage notes from 0.1M north of Knap Fl G 5s buoy (outside the western breakwater) to Mayflower Marina. It is HW–2 hrs.

13.4

You are the navigator of a yacht on passage from St Malo to Saint Quay-Portrieux at night. You wish to approach the harbour from the south from your present position 49° 12'.0N 05° 52'.0W. The height of tide is 3.8m and falling. Without remaining below at the chart table for extended periods, describe how you could:

    a) Plan to round Caffa Q (3) 10s light safely with a cross tide running.
    b) Clear the drying <u>3.7</u> metre rock La Roselière.
    c) Plan to approach the marina avoiding all dangers en route.

13.5

You are the skipper of a planing-hull motor cruiser on a cross-channel passage from Alderney to Fowey in daylight. Luck is definitely not with you because the visibility has fallen to under 0.5M and both your GPS and radar are inoperative. Your EP is 50° 15'.7N 05° 35'.7W with a circle of uncertainty, radius 1 mile. You decide to divert to Mevagissey. Wind is light SW and the tide is north-going. Explain:

    a) Possible reasons for the diversion to Mevagissey.
    b) Your strategy for approaching the harbour safely.

13.6

Describe a pilotage plan at 25kn from St Peter Port breakwater to St Helier harbour entrance, leaving the Lower Heads and Le Chats buoys to port and the two north cardinal marks close to the Jersey coast to starboard. Assume that the tidal stream is almost slack.

Turn to page 65-7 for answers

14. Meteorology

14.1

What are the meanings of the following terms used in weather bulletins?

a) fog   b) veering   c) falling   d) moving steadily
e) later   f) moderate   g) fair   h) imminent

14.2

Which Beaufort wind force would you expect for the following wind speeds and sea state?

a) 11 – 16 knots.   Small waves becoming larger. Frequent white crests.
b) 28 – 33 knots.   Sea heaps up, white foam, breaking waves blown into streaks.

14.3

What does Buys Ballot's Law tell you about the position of a low pressure area?

14.4

Draw a diagram to show how a sea breeze develops.

14.5

Sea fog is common in late spring and early summer in the English Channel. Why is this and what conditions will cause it to disperse?

14.6

The wind has been blowing strongly from a south-westerly direction for a number of days. What would be of particular significance to a yacht at sea if an occlusion then passed over the area with an accompanying sudden wind shift to the north west?

14.7

Use the weather map and associated forecast on page 31 to answer the following questions:

a) What would be the appearance of the sky in:
   1) Humber?   2) West Sole?
b) Why is the visibility forecasted to deteriorate in Dover? When will there be a marked improvement in visibility?
c) Why are the winds in the Thames and Humber areas expected to change by veering, whilst in the Irish Sea they are expected to change by backing?
d) If you were anchoring in area Forth, from which wind direction would you seek shelter?
e) Explain briefly the forecasts for Plymouth and for Lundy and Fastnet.

Turn to pages 68–9 for answers

Meteorology *continued*

SHIPPING FORECAST
Issued by the Meteorological Office at 1700 on Sunday 25 August.

There are warnings of gales in:
Forties, Cromarty, Forth, Tyne, Dogger, German Bight, Humber, Thames, Dover, Wight, Portland, Plymouth, Biscay, Finisterre, Sole, Lundy, Fastnet, Irish Sea, Shannon, Rockall, Malin.

General synopsis at 1300:   Vigorous low Fastnet 985 moving slowly north east with little change.

Area forecasts for the next 24 hours:

Viking, N & S Utsire	NW 4 veering E 5 or 6. Showers. Good.
Forties, Cromarty, Forth	E 3 increasing 7 to gale 8. Showers then rain. Good becoming moderate.
Tyne, Dogger	E 4 increasing 7 to severe gale 9. Rain. Good becoming poor.
Fisher, German Bight	Variable 3 becoming SE 7 to gale 8. Rain later. Good becoming poor.
Humber, Thames	SE 4 increasing 6 to gale 8 veering SW later. Rain. Moderate or poor.
Dover, Wight	SE 6 to gale 8 veering SW 7 to severe 9. Rain. Moderate or poor.
Portland	SE 6 to gale 8 veering SW 7 to severe 9. Rain. Moderate or poor becoming good.
Plymouth	SW 7 to severe gale 9 increasing storm 10 at times then veering NW. Rain. Moderate or poor becoming good.
Biscay	SW veering NW 5 or 6, but in north 6 to gale 8 occasionally severe gale 9. Occasional rain. Poor becoming good.
Finisterre, Sole	SW veering NW 7 to severe gale 9 occasionally storm 10 decreasing 5 in west later. Rain then showers. Poor becoming good.
Lundy, Fastnet	Cyclonic 7 to severe gale 9 increasing storm 10 at times then becoming northerly. Rain. Moderate or poor.
Irish Sea	E 7 to severe gale 9 perhaps storm 10 later. Rain. Moderate or poor.
Shannon	N gale 8 to storm 10 decreasing 6 to gale 8. Rain then showers. Moderate or poor.
Rockall, Malin	NE 7 to severe gale 9 backing N 6 to gale 8. Occasional rain. Moderate or good.
Hebrides, Bailey, F Isle	E 4 or 5 occasionally 6 in Hebrides. Showers. Good.
Faeroes, SE Iceland	Variable 3 becoming NW 4 or 5. Showers. Moderate or good.

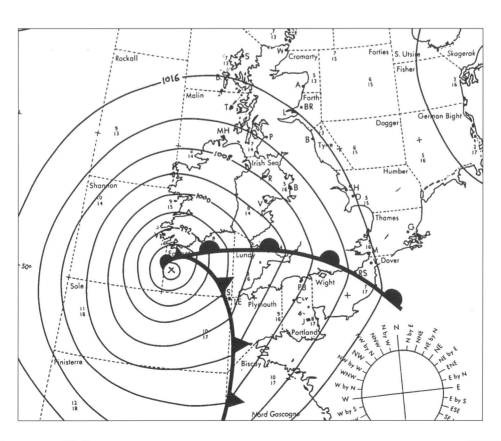

Turn to page 69 for answers

15. Passage Planning

Use chart RYA 1. Use extracts at the back of the book.

Questions 1, 2 and 5 use BST. Question 3 uses UT.
Passage planning does not always result in definitive answers; sometimes there is more than one sensible option.

15.1

You are the skipper of a motor yacht moored at a deep water mooring near Helford Village in the Helford River planning a passage to Looe on Sunday 14 April.
The forecast is for light and variable winds. Cruising speed 10kn.

    a) How far is the passage? What is the approximate passage time?
    b) Between what times on 14 April is Looe accessible?
    c) Between what times is the tidal stream favourable?
    d) Suggest an estimated time of departure and an estimated time of arrival and give reasons.
    e) What are the hazards   (i)   off Dodman Point?
                                (ii) off Looe Island?
                                (iii) in Looe Harbour?
       How could you ensure that you avoid these hazards without the use of electronic position fixing aids?
    f) How is the visitors' berth marked?

15.2

You are the skipper of a bilge keel yacht dried out on the visitors' berth in Looe. You are planning a passage via the Alderney Race to Dahouet to arrive on Friday 19 April. Forecast wind NE4 with good visibility. Estimated boat speed 5kn. HW St Malo 2030 BST.

    a) What is the length of the passage?
    b) Between what times (BST) can you leave Looe?
    c) Is Looe well enough lit to leave the harbour when it is dark? Give reasons for your answer.
    d) At what time should you aim to enter the Alderney Race and pass between Sark and Jersey?
    e) Is it safe to enter Dahouet with the forecast wind direction?
    f) Between what times is there access to Dahouet Marina?
    g) What will be your ETA at Dahouet? (It helps to estimate an ETA at the top of the race, abeam NW Jersey, at Les Landas north cardinal mark and Plateau des Jaunes.)
    h) Where could you anchor off Dahouet if you miss the marina opening times?
    i) What dangers are there *en route*?

Turn to page 70 for answers

Passage Planning *continued*

15.3

You are planning a passage from Cherbourg to Falmouth on Sunday 17 March. Wind is 290°(T) force 4, forecast to freshen and veer to NW6 by early afternoon. Boat speed close-hauled is 5kn. Tacking angle 90°.

a) How far is the passage (i) rhumb line distance?
                                      (ii) approximate distance tacking?
b) What is the best tacking strategy to make use of the forecast wind veer?
c) When should you depart?
d) When is your approximate ETA (UT)?

15.4

You are the skipper of a sailing yacht bound for Diélette. Your present position is 49° 57'.5N 05° 00'.0W. It has been a slow passage against a SSW 4–5 wind and the crew is looking forward to arriving and eating at their favourite restaurant. An electrical fault has meant that you have not received any weather forecasts since sailing. The weather is fine but, within the last few hours, streaky cirrus clouds have appeared and the sun has become hazy. You also notice that the barometer has fallen 4 millibars in the last 2 hours. What action, if any, should you take?

15.5

You are the skipper of a motor cruiser in the marina at Dahouet, intending to make a passage to Plymouth on Tuesday 9 April. You have 65 gallons of fuel. You were hoping to refuel in Dahouet, but none is available because it is a local holiday.

Fuel consumption is:	7kn, displacement	2.8 mpg
	12kn, wind against tide	2.0 mpg
	20kn, planing	1.2 mpg

Wind SW5   HW St Malo   1030 French Standard Time = BST

a) What is the distance of the passage?
b) Will you have to refuel?
c) What is your passage plan?

Turn to page 71 for answers

16. Passage Making

Use chart RYA 1. Variation 7°W. All times are given in BST.

In this exercise you are skipper of a 30ft yacht which draws 1.5m, will cruise at 5kn, and has a displacement of 5 tons. The forecast is for a fine day with winds W 3 to 4.

   You are currently moored in St Peter Port (Guernsey) outer harbour where there are no tidal height restrictions. The date is Monday 22 April. HW St Malo   0930 BST.

16.1

Prepare a passage plan from St Peter Port to Diélette on the French mainland using the Big Russel channel, and consider the following:

   a) Approximate distance from St Peter Port to Diélette and approximate duration of passage.
   b) Any restrictions concerning the arrival time at Diélette. (Use data for Flamanville.)
   c) Best time to leave St Peter Port for optimum tidal stream assistance.
   d) Dangers *en route*.

16.2

At 0737 the following bearings are taken when the log reads 63.4:

Noire Pute beacon (E side of Herm Island)	255°(M)
Bec du Nez Light on the north end of the Isle of Sark	201°(M)
Black and white beacon 1.1M north of Herm	292°(M)

Plot the 0737 fix.

16.3

Using the log extract below and the fix above, plot the EP at 0837.

Date	Time	Log	Course	Wind	Leeway	Baro	Notes
Mon 22	0737	63.4	100°(C)	S3	Nil	1030	Fix
April	0837	68.0	100°(C)	S3	Nil	1030	EP using ◇N

16.4

At 0937 the yacht is in position 49° 38'.0N 05° 10'.6W sailing at 5kn in a freshening south-easterly wind. Leeway is estimated at 5°.

   a) What is the compass course to steer to the west cardinal mark to the south west of Diélette? Use ◇M .

   b) At what time will the yacht cross the 20m contour?

16.5

Your propeller shaft is vibrating badly as you approach the marina and you fear that you will have to have the boat lifted out. Is this possible at Diélette?

Turn to pages 72–4 for answers

Part II

ANSWERS

1. Nautical Terms and Seamanship

1.1

1 P	5 C	9 I	13 G	17 H	21 E
2 R	6 D	10 S	14 B	18 O	22 A
3 X	7 J	11 U	15 N	19 W	23 T
4 Q	8 M	12 V	16 L	20 F	24 K

1.2

1 F	5 P	9 C	13 D
2 G	6 L	10 M	14 B
3 J	7 O	11 H	15 K
4 A	8 I	12 E	16 N

1.3

1 I	4 M	7 H	10 B	13 F
2 E	5 L	8 G	11 J	
3 D	6 C	9 K	12 A	

A 7	E 4
B 5	F 2
C 3	G 7
D 6	

1.4

A Bowline: For making a non slip loop in the end of a rope.

B Clove hitch: For securing the 'middle' of a rope to a spar. Both ends should be under load.

C Round turn and two half hitches: For securing a rope to a ring with minimum chafe. Can be released under load.

D Single sheet bend: For joining two ropes of unequal diameters.

E Reef knot: For reef points.

1.5

A Close hauled port tack.

B Close reach or fine reach port tack.

C Beam reach port tack.

D Broad reach port tack.

E Run goosewinged port tack.

Nautical Terms and Seamanship *continued*

1.6

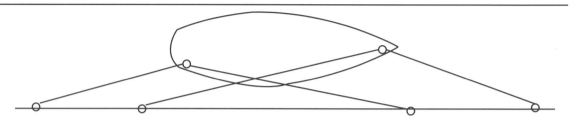

1.7

A	4	**D**	3
B	3	**E**	4
C	1	**F**	2

2. Chart Familiarisation

2.1

a) Chart datum.
b) Mean High Water Springs.

2.2

A magenta box drawn around the area covered by the larger scale chart 9219.
(*Note*: chart 9219 is a fictitious chart.)

2.3

a) Traffic Separation Scheme.
b) Areas that are uncovered at chart datum and covered at Mean High Water Springs (MHWS).
c) A navigational buoy that is lit.
d) Charted depth of between 10m and 20m, enclosed by a contour line.

2.4

a) Rock awash at chart datum.
b) Wreck considered to be dangerous to surface navigation.
c) Public slipway.
d) Tidal rips, overfalls.
e) Flagstaff.
f) Overhead cable with vertical clearance of 20m at MHWS.
g) Visitors' mooring.
h) Rock which covers and uncovers.
i) Windmill.
j) Ebb tide stream (with rate).

2.5

a) Rock and gravel.
b) Sand, shells and pebbles.
c) Coarse sand, broken shells, pebbles and mud.

2.6

a) Tidal diamond ⟨P⟩.
b) Recommended anchorage.
c) Submarine cable.
d) Spot height 80m above MHWS.

2.7

a) 101°(T) 6.4M
b) 268°(T) 24.2M
c) 330°(T) 4.5M
d) 172°(T) 13.1M

2.8

Ensure that the year and the correction numbers are entered on the bottom left-hand corner of the chart (in ink).

3. Compass

3.1

7° 25'.0W decreasing 6' annually. 7° 25'.0 – 18' = 7° 07'.0W.

3.2

  a) 085° (T)
  b) 193° (T)
  c) 003° (T)
  d) 354° (T)

3.3

  a) 260° (M)
  b) 006° (M)
  c) 003° (M)
  d) 355° (M)

3.4

Deviation is the error caused by the vessel's own magnetism. Ferrous items, particularly those that have been machined or hammered, gain a polarity which causes the ship's compass to deviate. The amount by which the compass is deviated depends on the heading of the vessel.

3.5

Probably heeling error. Measurements for deviation will have been taken with the boat on an even keel but the deviation may alter when the yacht is well heeled. Try checking your heading with the hand-bearing compass which can be deployed clear of magnetic influences.

3.6

True	Variation	Magnetic	Deviation	Compass
231°	6°W	237°	2°W	239°
079°	3°E	076°	0°	076°
147°	4°W	151°	1°E	150°
013°	2°E	011°	2°W	013°
348°	2°W	350°	1°E	349°

3.7

  a) Bearing of transit   069°(T)
        Variation   +7°W
  b) Magnetic   076°(M)
        Compass reads   072°(C)
  c) Deviation   4°E   (Compass reads less, so the deviation is east.)

4. Position Fixing

4.1

a) 49° 52'.6N   05° 29'.8W
b) 50° 13'.0N   05° 24'.1W

4.2

a) 50° 15'.4N   04° 59'.5W
b) 50° 17'.5N   05° 05'.9W
c) 50° 18'.0N   05° 13'.1W

This fix may be regarded as accurate particularly as bearings were taken to check that the conspicuous features were identified correctly. Both Penlee Point and Rame Head are steep-to and not too distant which assists accuracy. The depth check demonstrates that the craft was just to the south of the 30m sounding.

d) The cocked hat is centred on 50° 17'.1N   05° 35'.3W.   Use of the echo sounder will reveal whether you are closer to the 16m sounding at the southern side of the cocked hat or the 20+m sounding at the northern end.

e) Approx 50° 21'.3N   05° 24'.4W

The angle of cut is shallow and only two objects were used giving an inaccurate fix. The sounding does little to assist as a large area has a uniform sounding.

4.3

Distance off Casquets light	15.5M
Distance off Gros du Raz light	17.3M
Position	50° 03'.8N 05° 22'.6W

4.4

The yacht is probably crossing close to the end of the Casquets Separation Scheme and the horn heard is Channel West Lanby light float.

Approximate position is 49° 48'.8N   06° 03'.0W.

5. International Regulations for Preventing Collisions at Sea

5.1

  a) Keep as near to the outer limit of the channel as possible on your starboard side.
  b) Sailing vessels and vessels under 20m shall not impede the safe passage of a vessel which can safely navigate only within the channel.

5.2

  a) By watching the compass bearing of the approaching vessel. If the bearing does not change there is a risk of collision.
  b) By showing a different aspect of your lights to the other vessel.

5.3

  a) B should sound one short blast and turn to starboard to pass astern of A.
  b) A and B should both sound one short blast and both turn to starboard.
  c) B should avoid A. B may turn to port to avoid passing to windward of A.
  d) B on port tack should luff or gybe to avoid A.
  e) A, the windward vessel, should bear away behind B or tack.
  f) A, the windward vessel, should gybe and pass astern of B.

5.4

Heading.

5.5

  a) One long and two short blasts at intervals not exceeding two minutes.
  b) One long and two short blasts at intervals not exceeding two minutes.
  c) Two long blasts at intervals not exceeding two minutes.
  d) One long blast followed by four short blasts at intervals not exceeding two minutes.
  e) One long blast at intervals not exceeding two minutes.
  f) Bell for five seconds at not more than one minute intervals.
  g) One long and two short blasts at intervals not exceeding two minutes.
  h) One long and three short blasts at intervals not exceeding two minutes.

International Regulations for Preventing Collisions at Sea *continued*

5.6

a) Sailing vessel underway, under 20m in length, head on.
b) Power driven vessel underway, probably over 50m in length, starboard aspect.
c) Vessel towing, probably over 50m in length with tow under 200m, underway, starboard aspect.
d) A vessel engaged in fishing other than trawling underway, but not making way or at anchor. Any aspect, no gear extending more than 150m, any length.
e) A vessel at anchor probably over 50m in length but under 100m, starboard aspect *or* a power driven vessel probably over 50m underway, hull down or beyond visibility of side-lights, port aspect.
f) A vessel restricted in ability to manoeuvre engaged in underwater operations or dredging, stern aspect, making way, foul on its starboard side, any length.
g) Vessel not under command, underway but stopped, any aspect, any length.
h) Vessel constrained by its draught probably over 50m underway, port aspect.

5.7

No.

5.8

a) Not under command.
b) At anchor.
c) Engaged in fishing.
d) Restricted in ability to manoeuvre.

e) Constrained by draught.
f) Aground.
g) Motorsailing.

5.9

When overtaking.
When risk of collision occurs with a vessel:

- restricted in ability to manoeuvre
- not under command
- engaged in fishing
- which can only navigate safely in a narrow channel
- following a traffic lane in a Traffic Separation Scheme

When to windward of another yacht pointing higher on starboard tack.

6. Safety

6.1

Mayday, Mayday, Mayday.
This is yacht *Alpha*, yacht *Alpha*, yacht *Alpha*.
Mayday yacht *Alpha*.
My position is 180°(T) Start Point 3 miles.
Yacht is sinking. 4 persons abandoning to the liferaft.
Require immediate assistance. Over.

6.2

   a) Dry powder.
   b) Fire blanket.
   c) Halon or other gas extinguisher.

6.3

Allow the line to earth on the yacht or in the water. Take up the slack and pull when directed. Do not attach the line to the yacht. The winchman or diver will be lowered from the helicopter. The line steadies him and guides him to the yacht. The helmsman should concentrate on the course (as previously directed by the helicopter) and not be distracted. The winchman will take charge once on deck.

6.4

   a) When there is any likelihood of abandoning the yacht or going into the water.
      At all times for non-swimmers.
      In the dinghy.
   b) Depending on the experience of the crew, in rough seas and at all times at night.
   c) Jackstays, standing rigging, mast, cleats, rings and other strong points but not guardrails or running rigging.

6.5

   a) Orange smoke or pin point red.
   b) Pin point red.
   c) White parachute.

6.6

- Fix position.
- Hoist radar reflector.
- Switch on navigation lights.
- Put on lifejacket and harness. Make sure you can release harness quickly.
  (*Note:* The danger of falling overboard in fog is as great as not being able to unclip in a collision situation.)
- Post lookouts to listen and look.
- Head out of shipping channels.
- Sound fog horn.
- Use echo sounder and all other aids to plot position.
- Have white flares at hand.

7. Tidal Heights

7.1

1)	C	5)	D
2)	B	6)	F
3)	A	7)	E
4)	G		

7.2

a) MHWN Falmouth 4.2m + 2.1m = 6.3m
b) MLWS Goury 1.4m + 0.5m = 1.9m
c) MHWS Dahouet 11.3m – drying 5.5m = 5.8m
d) No. MLWN Alderney 2.5m – drying 2.4m = 0.1m depth.
e) Drying height 7.1m + draught 1.2m + clearance 0.3m = 8.6m
   MHWN St Malo = 9.2m
   The yacht can pass over with 0.6m to spare.
f) Yes, just. At MHWS Falmouth (5.3m) the mast hits the cable.
   Drop of at least 2m is required for clearance, therefore max tide height is 3.3m.
   Depth over drying 1m sounding with 3.3m tide = 2.3m.
   A brave (or foolish) navigator could attempt this but with only 0.3m total clearance.
   Another boat's wake could cause the mast to snag the cable or the keel to touch the bottom.

7.3

Between about 0545 and 0745 and between 1800 and 2000.

7.4

a)	0138 UT 0.3m	b)	1456 BST 4.3m	c)	0051 BST 0.8m
	0745 UT 5.8m		2051 BST 2.1m		0659 BST 5.3m

7.5

a)	2.2m, neaps	b)	11.4m, springs (and more)	c)	3.5m halfway

7.6

Height required   2.0m drying height
                  + 1.2m draught
                    3.2m

LW 0.6m   HW 1958 BST 5.3m, springs
From graph, tide will reach 3.2m at HW – 3 hrs 30 mins
The yacht will float at 1628 BST

45

Tidal Heights continued

7.7

HW 1337 UT   4.1m   LW 2.3m   neap range
1657 is HW + 3 hrs 20 mins
Height of tide 3.1m
Tide will fall 3.1m – 2.3m = 0.8m
              Draught   + 1.5m
                          _____
                           2.3m

Clearance = Depth – (Tidal fall + draught) = 2.7m – 2.3m = 0.4m

7.8

Plymouth HW	0554	5.5m	LW	1214	0.4m	HW	1816	5.5m
Corr. Par	–15	–0.4m		00	–0.2m		–15	–0.4m
Par BST	0639	5.1m		1314	0.2m		1901	5.1m

7.9

St Malo HW French Standard Time	1011	10.6m	LW	1652	3.0m	HW	2216	10.6m
Corr. Diélette		+50	–2.2m		+ 33	–0.8m		+50	–2.2m
Diélette French Summer Time	1201	8.4m		1825	2.2m	(22nd) 0006	8.4m

Using a halfway point between the two range curves, the graph shows that the height at + 4 hrs
10 mins is the same as at –3 hrs 10 mins. (Note that this transfer can only be done when the
ranges of the two tides are the same.) The yacht will refloat at 0006 – 3 hrs 10 mins = 2056
French Summer Time. The height of tide at this time is 4.7m.

7.10

HW Plymouth UT	2020	5.2m	LW	0.9m	Range 4.3m
Corr. Mevagissey	–18	–0.1m		–0.1m	(spring curve)
Mevagissey UT	2002	5.1m		0.8m	

From graph   Height of tide at 2242 (HW + 2 hrs 40 mins) = 3.65m
Tide will fall   3.65m – 0.8m = 2.85m
Minimum depth is   2.85m fall of tide
                                         +1.7m draught
                                         +1.0m clearance
                                         _____
                                          5.55m

7.11

a) High barometric pressure can depress tidal heights (by 0.3m if pressure is 34 mb above the
    mean of 1012 mb).

b) Low barometric pressure can result in tides higher than predicted, storms cause surges
    giving exceptionally high tides particularly in estuaries, the North Sea coast, and areas like
    the Bristol Channel where the land funnels.

8. Tidal Streams

8.1

a) 232°(T) 2.6kn	b) 045°(T) 0.9kn	c) 063°(T) 2.2sp 1.0np Int 1.6kn

8.2

a) 097°(T) 2.4kn	b) 220°(T) 2.0kn

8.3

19 April: HW Plymouth 0735 and 1952 BST. Range 5m and 4.9m, springs
Use tidal stream chartlets to note that the stream is NE-going until 4¹/₂ hours after HW Plymouth, ie 1205 BST. It would therefore be wise to complete the passage in a wind-with-tide situation when the sea will be flat enough for a motor cruiser.

At around 0930 BST there would be between 2¹/₂kn and 4kn of stream when the passage would be very uncomfortable or even harmful to the boat. It would therefore be prudent to delay the start until after lunch.

8.4

a)	20 January	HW 1744 UT	Range 4.9m, springs			
	◇J HW+1	1714 – 1814 UT	098°(T)	3.4kn		
b)	28 April	HW 1456 BST	Range 2.2m, neaps			
	◇G HW – 4	1026 – 1126 BST	241°(T)	1kn		
c)	11 February	HW 0935 UT	Range 3.5m, midway between springs and neaps.			
	◇H HW + 3	1205 – 1305 UT	039°(T)	3.2sp	1.4np	Int 2.3kn
d)	20 February	HW 0639 UT	Range 5.6m, super springs			
	TSA HW – 3	0309 – 0409 UT	205°(T)	5.7sp	2.3np	Ext 6.9kn
e)	11 March	HW 0920 UT	Range 3.8m			
	◇F HW – 3	0550 – 0650 UT	264°(T)	2.8sp	1.4np	Int 2.3kn
f)	17 April	HW 1835 BST	Range 5.0m, springs			
	◇C HW + 4	2205 – 2305 BST	055°(T)	1.0sp	0.5np	Ext 1.1kn
g)	21 February	HW 1950 UT	Range 5.5m, super springs			
	◇K HW – 5	1420 – 1520 UT	216°(T)	5.3sp	2.5np	Ext 6.2kn

Tidal Streams *continued*

8.5

a) HW 0429 BST. Stream west-going HW Plymouth $+1^{1}/_{2}$ hrs = 0700 French Summer Time
b) HW 1526 UT.   Stream north-going HW Plymouth $-1^{1}/_{2}$ hrs = 1500 French Standard Time

8.6

The stream runs more slowly when it is shallow close to the shore, particularly where the bottom
shelves gradually as it does in the Baie de Saint-Brieuc. Grand Léjon lighthouse is situated in water
of approximately 20m and is on a line joining headlands and rocky outcrops. Streams inshore
could well be half the rate of the offshore streams but are likely to change direction earlier.

8.7

a) Tidal stream atlas.
b) Tidal diamonds.
c) Tidal stream atlas.

9. Estimated Position

9.1

EP 50° 11'.1N 04° 44'.9W

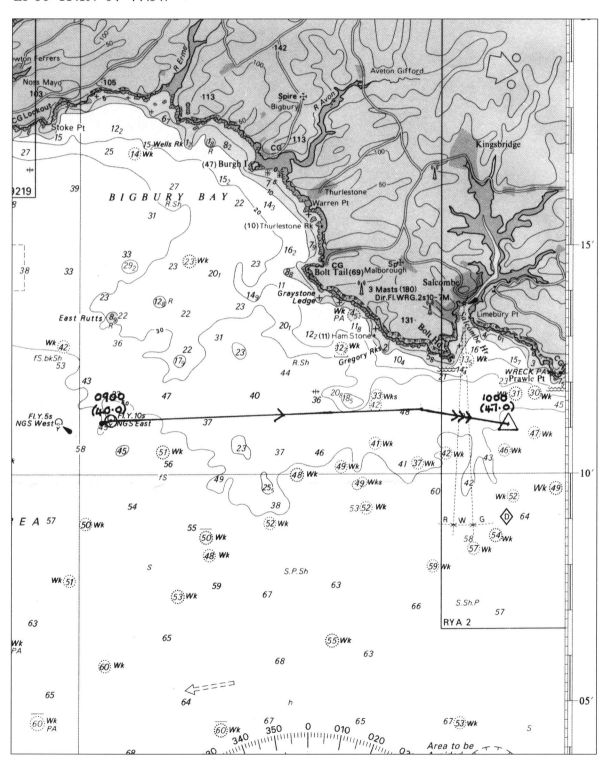

Estimated Position continued

9.2

Tidal stream 23 February 0844 UT   Range 4.8m

Ⓒ HW + 1   0914–1014 UT   083°(T)   2.2kn

EP 50° 13'.0N 05° 08'.8W

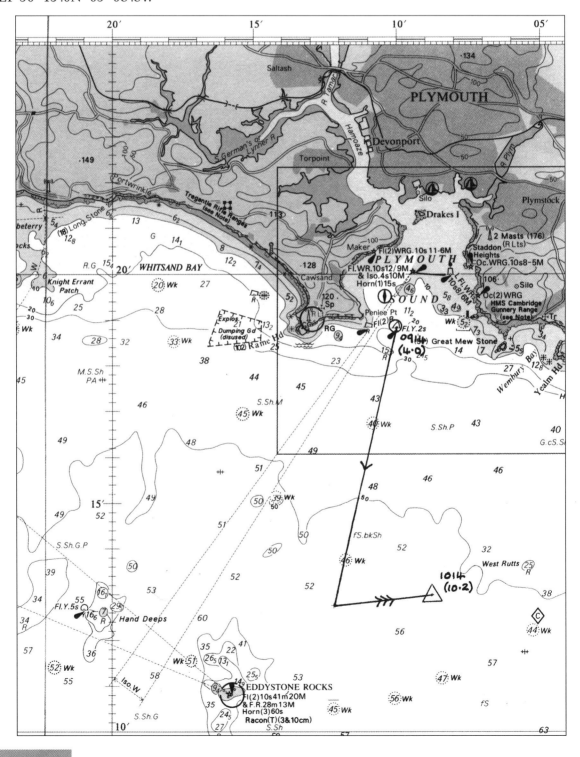

Estimated Position continued

9.3

Tidal streams	28 April		HW 1456 BST	Range 2.2m, neaps

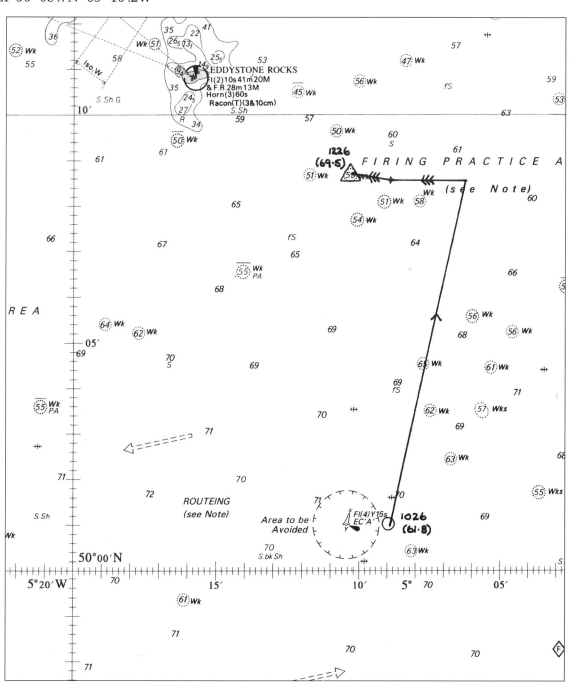

◇ F HW –4   1026–1126 BST   270°(T)   1.7kn

◇ C HW –3   1126–1226 BST   279°(T)   0.8kn

EP 50° 08'.7N 05° 10'.2W

Estimated Position continued

9.4

| Tidal streams | 6 April | HW 0816 BST | Range 4.7m, springs |

F HW + 5   1246–1346 BST   116°(T)   0.6kn

Course   260°(M)
Variation   −7°
                  ─────
                  253°(T)
Leeway   −10°
                  ─────
                  243°(T)

Course over the ground (COG) 237°(T). Speed over the ground (SOG) 4.9kn
EP 50° 00'.6N 04° 53'.5W

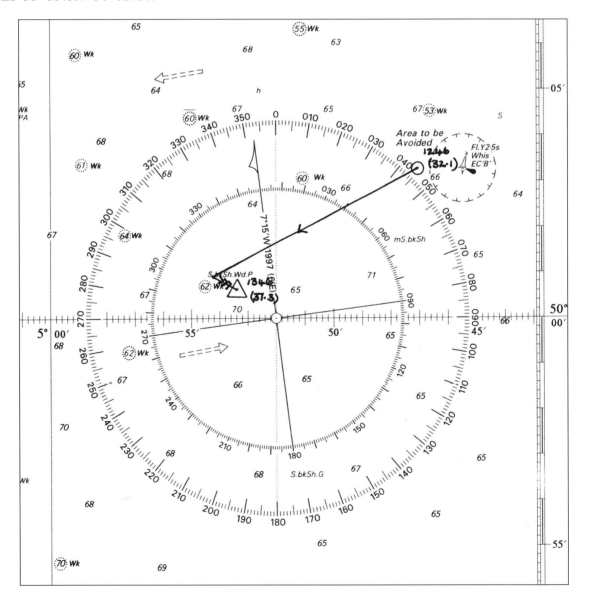

Estimated Position continued

9.5

Tidal streams   4 March   HW 1830 French Standard Time (UT+1)   Range 4.1m

◇ J   HW – 5   1300–1400 FStT   278°(T)   3.3sp   1.6np   Int 2.9kn

◇ J   HW – 4   1400–1500 FStT   280°(T)   2.5sp   1.2np   Int 2.2kn

EP 49° 56'.6N 04° 56'.2W Approximately 0.5M from Cherbourg Fairway buoy.

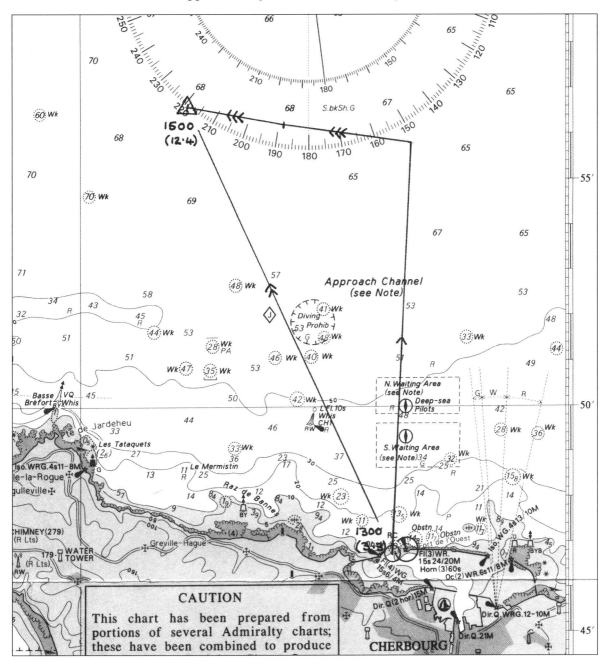

Estimated Position continued

9.6

First course	152°(C)		Second course	210°(C)
Deviation	+5°E		Deviation	+1°E
	157°(M)			211°(M)
	150°(T)		(No leeway)	204°(T)
Leeway	+10°			
	160°(T)			

Tidal streams   14 April   HW 1607 BST   Range 3.4m

⟨H⟩ HW – 3   1237–1337 BST   220°(T)   2.3sp   1.0np   Int 1.6kn

⟨H⟩ HW – 2   1337–1437 BST   212°(T)   0.8sp   0.3np   Int 0.5kn

EP 49° 48'.9N 05° 40'.8W

Note that the heading of 150°(T) is at right angles to the Traffic Separation Scheme.

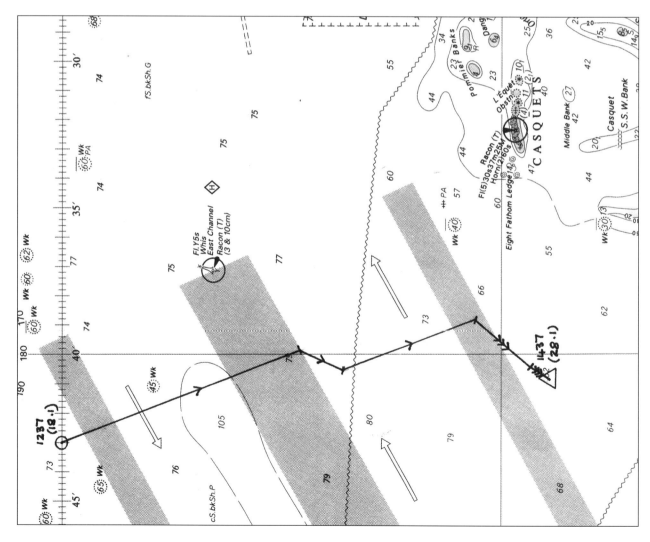

Estimated Position continued

9.7

Projected EP:	Course	114°(C)
		119°(M)
		112°(T)
	Leeway	+10°
		122°(T)

Tidal stream   20 March   0618 UT   Range 5.6m

⟨E⟩ HW + 2   0748–0848   061°(T)   1.4sp   0.7np   Ext 1.7kn

Plot EP for 0848 then draw the ground track. Draw a line parallel to the tide from the point at which the ground track meets the Traffic Separation Scheme to the water track. Measure log distance along the water track.
Log will read 21.8 + 3.9 = 25.7

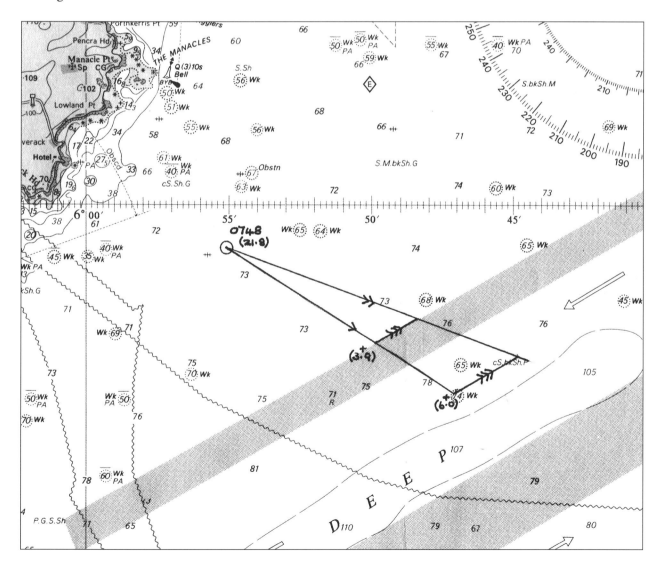

10. Buoyage and Lights

10.1

The broad magenta arrow on the Cornish coast Near Lizard Point shows the direction as SW to NE.

10.2

10.3

To starboard as it is a North Cardinal mark.

10.4

a) Port	b) Either side	c) Starboard	d) Either side
e) Starboard	f) Port	g) Starboard	

10.5

Flashing 2 white every 10 seconds plus a fixed red light.

10.6

No, the actual light would not be visible from the cockpit of a small yacht as the curvature of the earth would preclude this. The figure given (28M) is the nominal range, it assumes that the earth is flat and that the visibility is at least 10M. From the Dipping Distance table (on page 76)

Height of eye	2m
Height of light	37m
Max range	15.6M

10.7

a) St Martin's Point, Guernsey	b) Cap de Carteret	c) Point Robert, Sark
d) Carteret breakwater	e) Pierre de Herpin (NW corner Baie du Mont Saint-Michel)	f) Point du Roc, Granville

11. Course to Steer

11.1

a) 041°(T) + 7°W = 048°(M)   b) 6.6kn

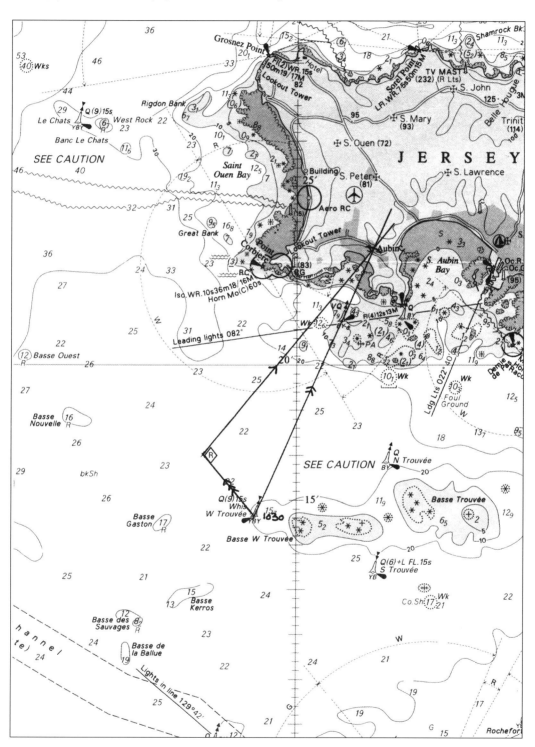

Course to Steer *continued*

11.2

HW 1900 Springs:

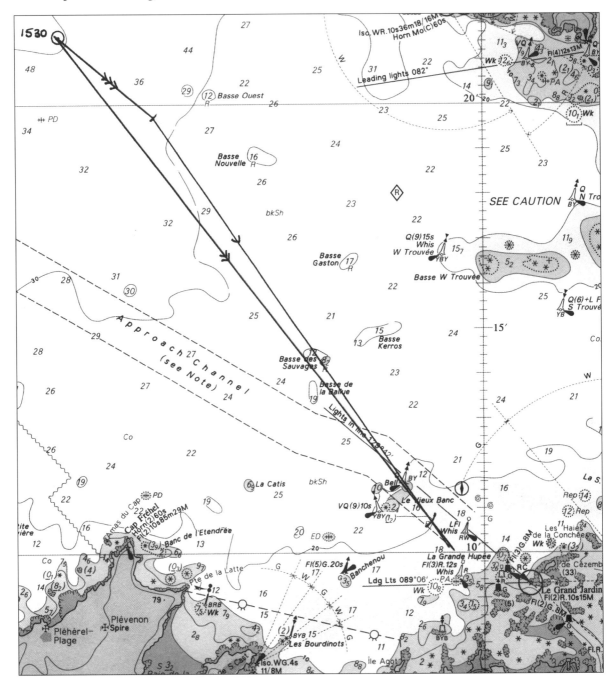

⟨R⟩ HW – 3   1530 – 1630   129°(T) 2.8kn

   a) 145°(T) = 152°(M)
   b) 13.8kn
   c) <u>Distance to travel</u> x 60 = <u>12.7</u> x 60 = 55 mins passage time. ETA = 1530 + 55 mins = 1625
      Speed over the ground   13.8

Course to Steer continued

11.3

23 March HW 0813 UT   Range 4.7m, springs

◇Q HW + 3   1043 – 1143 UT   283°(T) 1.9kn

Course to steer 183°(T) = 190°(M)

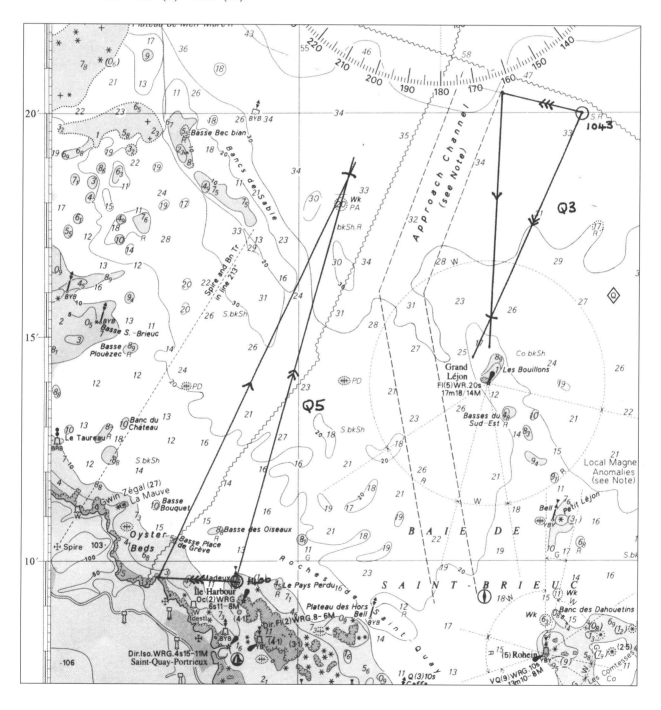

Course to Steer continued

11.4

25 April   HW   1057   BST   Range 2.2m, neaps

R   HW + 3   1327 – 1427 BST   310°(T)   1.0kn

Course to steer 172°(T) = 179°(M) – 4°E = 175°(C)

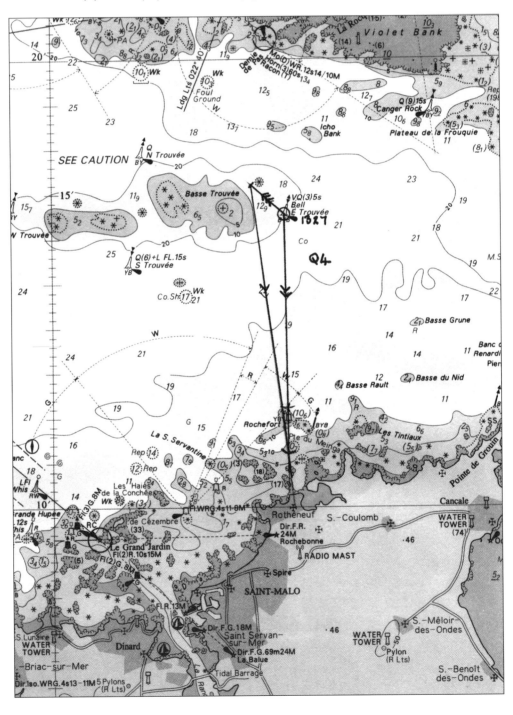

Course to Steer *continued*

11.5

24 January HW Plymouth 0930 French Standard Time Range 5.3m

◇ HW + 5   1400 – 1500 FStT   273°(T) 1.5sp 0.7np Ext 1.7kn

Course to steer 026°(T) = 033°(M) + 1°W = 034°(C)   See page 59 for chartwork.

11.6

9 April HW Plymouth 2228 BST Range 3.7m

◇ HW – 1   2058 – 2158   063°(T) 2.2sp 1.0np Int 1.7kn

◇ HW   2158 – 2258   055°(T) 2.3sp 1.0np Int 1.8kn

◇ HW + 1   2258 – 2358   045°(T) 2.0sp 0.9np Int 1.6kn

a) Course to steer 156°(T) = 163°(M) – 5° E = 158°(C)

b) $\frac{9.7}{15}$ x 180 mins = 116 mins = 1 hr 56 mins therefore buoy passed at 2256 BST

c) 156°(T) = 163°(M) + 5° leeway = 168°(M) – 5°E = 163°(C)

See page 62 for chartwork.

Course to Steer continued

11.6

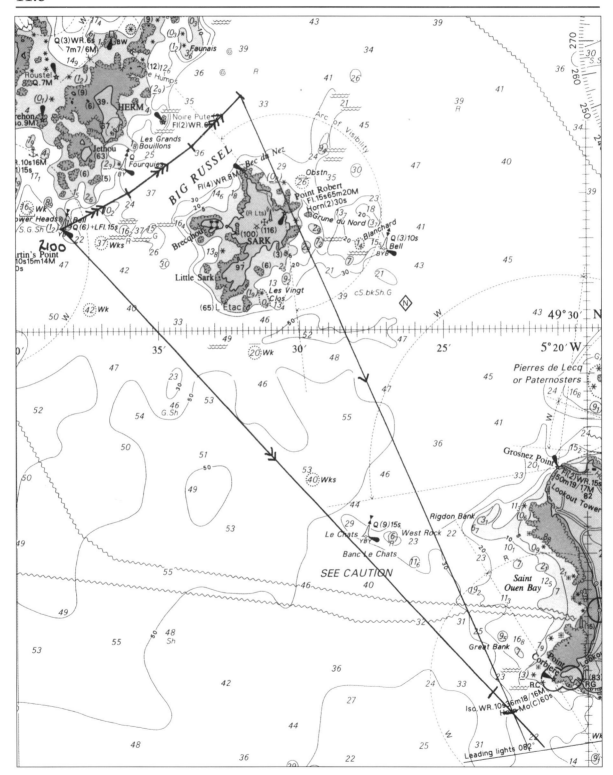

Course to Steer continued

11.7

13 April HW 1457 BST Range 2.8m

⟨L⟩ HW – 2   1227 – 1327   098°(T) 3.4sp 1.5np Int 2.0kn

a) Fix 49° 34'.0N 05° 57'.6W (approximately).

The navigator has sensibly taken four bearings because of the small angle of cut between bearings, but the bearings cross in a very small area. The headland is over 10 miles away, and even the lighthouse is over 4 miles which could result in inaccuracies. Two transits were obtained and as long as the features were identified correctly the fix could be more reliable than it first appeared.

b) Course to steer 135°(T) = 142°(M) + 10° leeway = 152°(M) – 5°E = 147°(C)

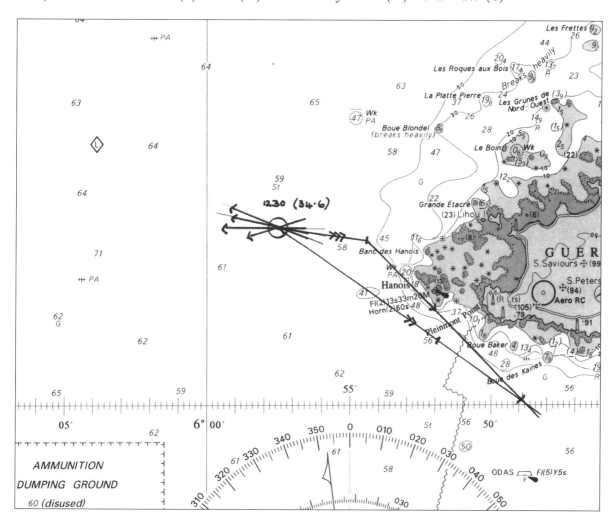

12. Navigational Instruments

12.1

The datum used for the GPS satellite positions may differ from the chart's positional datum. Look for a note near the title of most Admiralty charts.

12.2

a) A position fixing instrument such as GPS can be programmed with waypoints, ie with latitudes and longitudes of positions where a course will change, such as buoys and off headlands. A digital display will inform the navigator of the bearing and distance of the waypoint from the yacht's present position. Some navigators waypoint the centre of the compass rose on the chart which allows a quick and simple plot of the yacht's position.

b) The computer in most electronic navigation units knows the direct track from one waypoint to the next or from a defined position to a pre-entered destination. At any time it can tell the navigator if the yacht is off track. It will also advise as to which side of the track she is currently situated and which way to steer to bring her back on line to correct her cross track error.

12.3

It is quicker to shape a course. By following the rhumb line you will spend a significant part of the passage pointing slightly into the tide. On a 12 hour passage the tidal stream effect as predicted on a course to steer should sweep you off the line and then back to it, allowing the yacht to make the passage with minimal reduction in speed because of the tide.

12.4

The MOB function will bring you back to the geographical position where the person fell. You should now start to search in the direction the tidal stream is flowing. If the person is not immediately recovered, send a Mayday call.

12.5

The Dutchman's log involves dropping a chip of wood overboard at the bow and timing how long it takes to reach the stem. A nautical mile is 6080ft.

13. Pilotage

13.1

To port.

13.2

Plan to pass between Alderney and the rock. Use a clearing bearing of 022°(M) from the eastern edge of Burhou Island to clear the rock. If the right-hand edge (RHE) of Burhou bears more than 030°(M) then the yacht will be in danger. When the chimney on the SW corner of Alderney bears less than 077°(M), then the rock has been passed safely.

13.3

- Listen on Channel 14.
- Watch for ferries and RN ships near the breakwater and in the Sound.
- Best remain outside deep water channel on its western side, so steer 345°(M) to leave Fl(2) R 10s buoy close to starboard.
- At buoy alter course to 040°(M) and maintain for 0.75M.
- Tidal stream will be setting through the bridge channel so be wary of set onto the posts.
- At QG light alter course to 339°(M), then leave QR to port.
- In approximately 1 cable Fl (3) G to starboard and Fl (4) R to port.
- Stay in white sector of the Narrows Dir. WGR light until past QG light on Devil's Point.
- Keep land close to starboard until marina entrance is reached.

13.4

Use chart RYA 1 and Extract on page 81

a) The secret here is to use the white sector of Grand Léjon light and a clearing bearing of 205°(M) on Caffa. The bearing on Caffa can be checked by using the limit of the white arc of Grand Léjon light on its western side. Maintain the course until Rohein light changes from red to white.

b) Identify Binic harbour entrance Oc (3) 12s light and alter course to keep it on a steady bearing of 255°(M) for a distance of 2M. Whilst maintaining this track, identify the Dir. Iso WRG light on St Quay harbour wall.

c) When in the white sector of the light, turn onto a heading to maintain a ground track of 325°(M) to remain in the white sector of St Quay breakwater light.

13.5

a) Mevagissey approach is clear of offlying dangers, the depth contours are well defined close to the coast and there is a 12M powerful light on the breakwater. The fog horn could be in use to assist pilotage. In a light SW wind it would be safe and comfortable to anchor near the harbour or in the lee of the land if the harbour is not located. Fowey has Cannis Rock to the west of the entrance, ill defined depth contours and would be exposed to the SW wind if it were necessary to anchor off the harbour.

b) Select a safe cruising speed of perhaps 4kn or 5kn, then steer 295°(M) to a point downtide of Mevagissey. When the 10m contour is reached, turn onto 202°(M) and motor southwards, watching the echo sounder carefully to remain between the 10m and 5m contours. This approach into tide will give good control over ground speed on the final run towards the pier.

Pilotage *continued*

13.6

- Take a departure from St Peter Port harbour entrance.
- Shape a course to a position 1 mile off Corbière light. Bearing 135°(T) Distance 17M.
- Distance to Lower Heads south cardinal buoy = 2.4M. Track passes within 2 cables of the buoy.
- Distance to Le Chats west cardinal buoy = 12.2M. Track passes within 2 cables of the buoy.
- Watch for lobster pots in vicinity.
- Check distance off Corbière light 1M by radar or by headlands on south coast of Jersey in transit.
- Steer 099°(T) to pass between headlands and the north cardinal buoys.
- When Fl(4) 12s 13M light abeam to port steer 080°(T) until entrance bears 020°(T).
- Slow down and enter by eye.
- Passage time = 1 hour approximately.
- Note: 1 cable = 200yds approx.

Pilotage continued

13.6

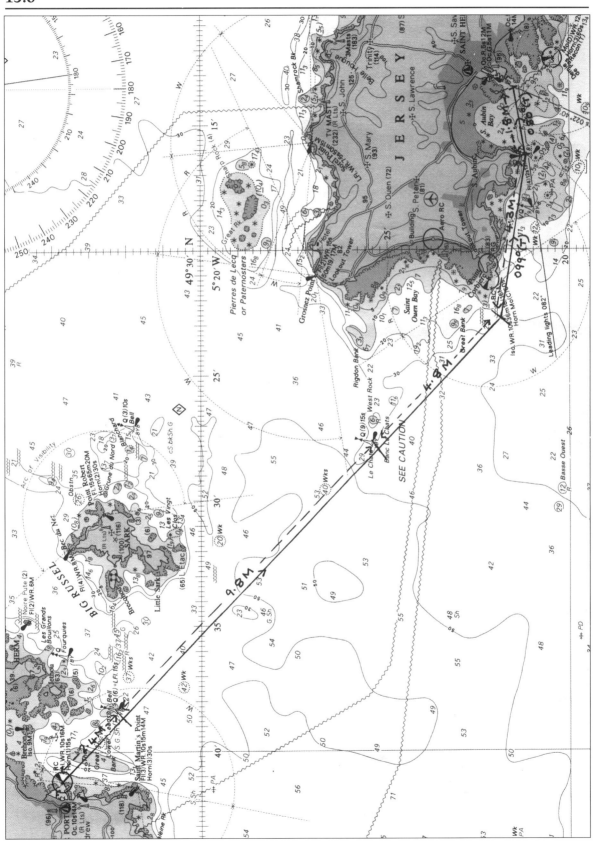

14. Meteorology

14.1

a) Visibility of less than 1100 yards (1000 metres).
b) A clockwise change in wind direction.
c) Pressure change of 1.6 to 3.5 millibars in the last three hours.
d) System moving at 15 to 25 knots.
e) After 12 hours from the time of issue.
f) Visibility of 2 to 5 nautical miles.
g) Nothing significant ie no showers, rain, mist.
h) Within 6 hours from the time of issue of the warning.

14.2

a) F4   b) F7

14.3

Buys Ballot's Law states, 'If you stand with your back to the wind in the northern hemisphere, low pressure will be on your left hand and high pressure on your right.'

14.4

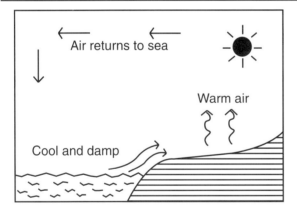

14.5

Sea fog (advection fog) forms when damp tropical maritime air is cooled as it blows over a cold surface. In the spring and early summer warm tropical air comes in from the warmer south but the sea remains cold until later in the summer. Sea fog occurs most frequently in winds of Beaufort F2 to F4 but can, on occasions, persist in winds of F5 or even F6. A change to a colder airstream will disperse this type of fog or stronger winds will lift it off the surface to simulate low stratus cloud.

14.6

As the wind has been blowing strongly in one direction for a few days a consistent wave pattern will have become established. A sudden windshift will cause confused seas and possibly dangerously high 'pyramid' waves. The weather is also likely to be squally.

Meteorology *continued*

14.7

a) Humber: High cirrus cloud with a possible halo around the sun. The cloud will gradually thicken and become lower as the warm front approaches.
West Sole: Good visibility with a few cumulus causing showers.

b) As the warm front approaches Dover, the cloud cover will become lower. As the front passes the rain and increasing humidity will cause poor visibility and there may be fog in the warm sector. When the cold front passes there will be a marked improvement in the visibility.

c) Thames and Humber will be south of the depression. Irish Sea will be north of the depression.

d) Shelter from the east and north are required.

e) Plymouth: The passage of the cold front will cause the wind to veer, the visibility to improve and the rain to become showery.
Lundy and Fastnet: The cyclonic wind occurs near the centre of the low. The isobars are close together therefore the wind will be strong. As the low moves east the wind becomes northerly.

15. Passage Planning

15.1

a) 30M approximately. 3 hrs' run.

b) 14 April HW Plymouth 1607 BST Range 3.4m
HW Looe is at 1557 BST
Access approx HW ± 1½ hours = 1430 to 1730.

c) Stream favourable for HW Plymouth – 1½ hrs to HW + 4½ hrs, ie 1430 – 2030.

d) It is best to decide the optimum time of arrival first, then work backwards for the ETD. Arrival time is critical because of the depths in the harbour, so aim to arrive 1M off the harbour entrance by 1430. It will be necessary to punch a foul stream up the coast from Helford but the streams are weak halfway between springs and neaps and with a boat speed of 10 knots this should not be a problem. Allowing an extra ¼ hour for the stream gives a departure time of 1115.

e) (i) Overfalls. Remain south of the 50m contour and close to the yellow buoys.
   (ii) Overfalls. Remain south of the 20m contour until Looe Banjo pier head bears less than 322°(M).
   (iii) Stream may well be running hard into the harbour giving poor boat control.

f) Visitors' berth is marked in yellow on the west side of the harbour.

15.2

a) 84M.

b) 19 April HW Plymouth 0735 BST 5.5m and 1952 5.4m. Range 5.0m and 4.9m, springs.
HW Looe 0735 BST – 10 minutes = 0725 BST
Access to Looe HW± 1½ hrs = 0600 – 0900 approx.

c) Yes. Use the white sector of Banjo Pier light to clear possible overfalls off Looe Island and use a bearing on Eddystone 20M light which should be clearly visible above the horizon at 12M (dips 16.2M).

d) Best to be at the top of the Alderney Race at HW Plymouth + 4½ hrs = 1200 BST (using tidal stream atlas). Be through the Sark/Jersey gap by HW Plymouth – 3 hrs = 1700 BST.

e) Yes – it will have a lee from the land.

f) Access to Dahouet Marina is HW Dahouet ± 2 hrs.
HW Dahouet = HW St Malo – 6 mins = 2024 BST.
Access is 1824 to 2224 BST.

g) Top of Race 1200 BST.
Abeam Grosnez point, Jersey 1500 BST, Corbière lighthouse 1600 BST, Les Landas north cardinal mark 1900 BST, Plateau des Jaunes 2000 BST, Dahouet 2030 BST.

h) Just north of Dahouet off the Val André beach.

i) Overfalls off Looe.
Shipping at around 50°N funnelling into the TSS off Casquets.
Paternoster Rocks off Jersey.
Magnetic anomalies between Le Grand Lèjon and Rohein (see note on chart RYA 1)
Rocky areas to the east of Rohein lighthouse.
Unlit post off Plateau des Jaunes.
Dahouet Rock and unlit NCM.
(*Note:* It could be more prudent to pass west of Rohein and approach the port from the NW.)

Passage Planning continued

15.3

17 March. HW Plymouth 0350 UT 5.2m and 1624 UT 5.1m.

a) (i) 49M rhumb line from Cherbourg harbour entrance to St Anthony lighthouse.
   (ii) 65 – 70M tacking.
b) You should depart on port tack to be on the English side in time for the veer. This would also put you in the lee when the wind freshens.
c) You should cross the Channel on the west going tidal stream (0900–1430) and take the foul weaker streams once closer to Falmouth, therefore leave at 0900 UT.
d) Approximate ETA 1730 UT.

15.4

A low pressure system is approaching. The wind is likely to veer and will probably strengthen from the west or north-west. The pilot book advises that entry into Diélette should not be made in strong westerlies and it may well be blowing hard by the time you arrive. The Alderney Race could be very uncomfortable if the wind pipes up quickly. Your best option is to divert to Cherbourg which is well sheltered, and convince the crew that there is an even better restaurant there.

15.5

a) 87M marina to marina.

b) You will have to refuel on the way. The best port at which to refuel is St Peter Port which is 31 miles away and as the main commercial port on the island is sure to have fuel.

c) HW St Malo   1030 French Standard Time = BST
    HW Dahouet   = HW St Malo – 6 mins = 1024 BST

Access to Dahouet marina is HW ± 2 hrs so craft could leave between 0824 and 1224.
HW Plymouth 1012 BST Range 3.7m.
Distance to Guernsey is 31M and the stream is more or less with the wind at 0824 when departing Dahouet. It may be possible to plane at 20kn, but 2½ hrs should be allowed for the passage to Guernsey.
   Fuelling should be completed as soon as possible so that the maximum wind-with-tide period can be used for planing at 20kn, giving Casquets a wide berth and observing the Traffic Separation Rules.
   From St Peter Port it is 56 miles to the marina at Plymouth and the passage should be possible keeping a favourable stream. It may be necessary to slow down nearer the Devon coast if there is any delay and the stream goes foul. Streams are weaker on the English side, so the sea should be calmer.

16. Passage Making

16.1

a) Approximately 28M.   Duration 5 hrs approximately.

b) 22 April   HW Plymouth   0907 BST   5.0m   Range 3.8m
                     HW Diélette = HW St Malo + 50 mins = 1020 BST

Diélette marina has access for 1.5m draught at HW ± 3 hrs approx = 0720 to 1320 approx

c) Streams are strong in this area, particularly at springs, so best to be at Lower Heads buoy when the stream begins to flow NE. From tidal stream atlas be at buoy at HW Plymouth – 2½ hrs, ie 0637, so leave St Peter Port harbour at 0600.

d) Overfalls at southern end of Herm and on the northern end of Sark.
   Rocky outcrops to NE of Herm.
   Rocky reef NE of Diélette entrance.
   Local magnetic anomalies (see note on chart RYA 1).

Passage Making continued

16.2

Fix 49° 35'.6N 05° 31'.2W

16.3

22 April   HW Plymouth   0907 BST   Range 4.0m.

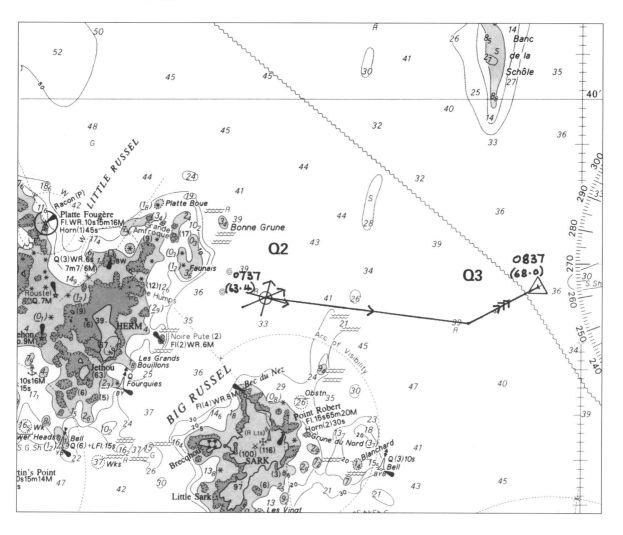 HW – 1   0737 – 0837   063°(T)   2.2 sp   1.0 np   Int 1.8kn.

Course	100°(C)
Deviation	+4°E
Magnetic	104°(M)
Variation	–7°W
	097°(T)

EP 49° 35'.9N 05° 21'.6W

Passage Making *continued*

16.4

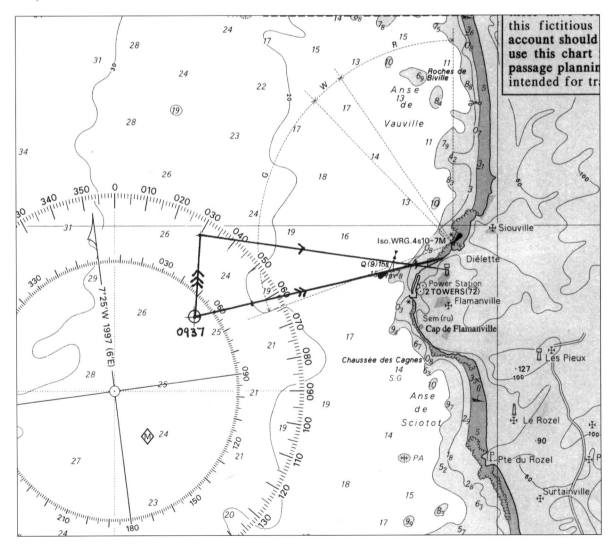

⬦M̂ HW + 1 0937–1037   004°(T)   2.3 sp   0.9 np   Int 1.8kn

a) Course   098°(T)
                                   +7°W
                                  105°(M)
    Leeway   +5°
                                  110°(M)
    Deviation   –5°E
    Course to steer   105°(C)

b) <u>Distance to 20m contour 1.4M</u> x 60 = 16 mins elapsed time = 0937 + 16 mins = 0953 BST
    Speed over the ground   5.2kn

16.5

Yes, there is a 10 ton crane.

Part III

EXTRACTS

Lights – distance off when rising or dipping (M)

Height of light			Height of eye									
metres	feet	metres	1	2	3	4	5	6	7	8	9	10
		feet	3	7	10	13	16	20	23	26	30	33
10	33		8·7	9·5	10·2	10·8	11·3	11·7	12·1	12·5	12·8	13·2
12	39		9·3	10·1	10·8	11·4	11·9	12·3	12·7	13·1	13·4	13·8
14	46		9·9	10·7	11·4	12·0	12·5	12·9	13·3	13·7	14·0	14·4
16	53		10·4	11·2	11·9	12·5	13·0	13·4	13·8	14·2	14·5	14·9
18	59		10·9	11·7	12·4	13·0	13·5	13·9	14·3	14·7	15·0	15·4
20	66		11·4	12·2	12·9	13·5	14·0	14·4	14·8	15·2	15·5	15·9
22	72		11·9	12·7	13·4	14·0	14·5	14·9	15·3	15·7	16·0	16·4
24	79		12·3	13·1	13·8	14·4	14·9	15·3	15·7	16·1	16·4	17·0
26	85		12·7	13·5	14·2	14·8	15·3	15·7	16·1	16·5	16·8	17·2
28	92		13·1	13·9	14·6	15·2	15·7	16·1	16·5	16·9	17·2	17·6
30	98		13·5	14·3	15·0	15·6	16·1	16·5	16·9	17·3	17·6	18·0
32	105		13·9	14·7	15·4	16·0	16·5	16·9	17·3	17·7	18·0	18·4
34	112		14·2	15·0	15·7	16·3	16·8	17·2	17·6	18·0	18·3	18·7
36	118		14·6	15·4	16·1	16·7	17·2	17·6	18·0	18·4	18·7	19·1
38	125		14·9	15·7	16·4	17·0	17·5	17·9	18·3	18·7	19·0	19·4
40	131		15·3	16·1	16·8	17·4	17·9	18·3	18·7	19·1	19·4	19·8
42	138		15·6	16·4	17·1	17·7	18·2	18·6	19·0	19·4	19·7	20·1
44	144		15·9	16·7	17·4	18·0	18·5	18·9	19·3	19·7	20·0	20·4
46	151		16·2	17·0	17·7	18·3	18·8	19·2	19·6	20·0	20·3	20·7
48	157		16·5	17·3	18·0	18·6	19·1	19·5	19·9	20·3	20·6	21·0
50	164		16·8	17·6	18·3	18·9	19·4	19·8	20·2	20·6	20·9	21·3
55	180		17·5	18·3	19·0	19·6	20·1	20·5	20·9	21·3	21·6	22·0
60	197		18·2	19·0	19·7	20·3	20·8	21·2	21·6	22·0	22·3	22·7
65	213		18·9	19·7	20·4	21·0	21·5	21·9	22·3	22·7	23·0	23·4
70	230		19·5	20·3	21·0	21·6	22·1	22·5	22·9	23·2	23·6	24·0
75	246		20·1	20·9	21·6	22·2	22·7	23·1	23·5	23·9	24·2	24·6
80	262		20·7	21·5	22·2	22·8	23·3	23·7	24·1	24·5	24·8	25·2
85	279		21·3	22·1	22·8	23·4	23·9	24·3	24·7	25·1	25·4	25·8
90	295		21·8	22·6	23·3	23·9	24·4	24·8	25·2	25·6	25·9	26·3
95	312		22·4	23·2	23·9	24·5	25·0	25·4	25·8	26·2	26·5	26·9
metres	feet	metres	1	2	3	4	5	6	7	8	9	10
Height of light		feet	3	7	10	13	16	20	23	26	30	33
							Height of eye					

MEVAGISSEY

CHARTS
AC 147, 148, 1267; Imray C6; Stanfords 13; OS 204

Standard Port DEVONPORT (→)

Times				Height (metres)			
High Water		Low Water		MHWS	MHWN	MLWN	MLWS
0000	0600	0000	0600	5.5	4.4	2.2	0.8
1200	1800	1200	1800				
Differences MEVAGISSEY							
−0015	−0020	−0010	−0005	−0.1	−0.1	−0.2	−0.1

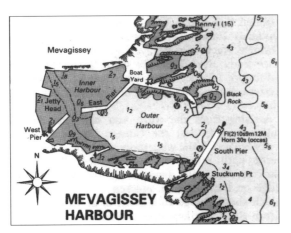

SHELTER
Exposed to E'lies, but available at all states of the tide. Dangerous to appr in strong SE'lies. V berth on S Quay in about 1.6m (D available). Bilge keelers/cats may dry out on sandy beach, SE side of W Quay. One visitors mooring in Outer hbr on request to Hr Mr. Anchoring inside the hbr is prohib due to over-crowding and many FVs. Anchoring outside the S Pier is only advised in settled weather with no E in the wind. Inner hbr (dries 1.5m) is reserved for FVs, unless taking on FW.

NAVIGATION
090°/270° from/to pier hd lt, 0.20M. Beware rky ledges off the N Quay. Hbr ent is 46m wide. Speed limit in the hbr is 3kn. Beware FVs.

LIGHTS AND MARKS
S Quay Fl (2) 10s 9m 12M, Horn (1) 30s (fishing).

RADIO TELEPHONE
Hr Mr VHF Ch 16 14 (Summer 0900-2100LT. Winter 0900- 1700LT); call on 16 for berth.

TELEPHONE (Dial code 01726)
Hr Mr 843305, (home 842496); MRSC (01803) 882704;

Customs 0345231110 (H24); Marinecall 0891 500458;

Police 842262; Dr 843701.

FACILITIES
Outer Hbr AB (S Quay) £5, M, FW, D; **Inner Hbr** Slip, FW, C (1 ton). **Service:** BY, Sh (wood), CH. **Village** EC Thurs; V,R, Gas, Bar, Ice.

FOWEY

CHARTS
AC 31, 148, *1267*; Imray C6, Y52; Stanfords 13; OS 204

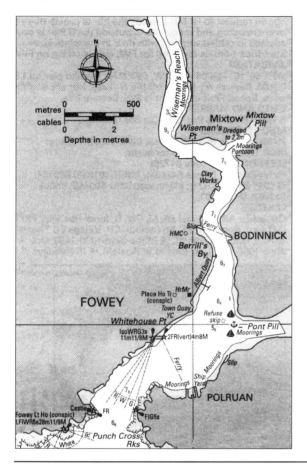

Standard Port PLYMOUTH (→)

Times				Height (metres)			
High Water		Low Water		MHWS	MHWN	MLWN	MLWS
0000	0600	0000	0600	5.5	4.4	2.2	0.8
1200	1800	1200	1800				
Differences FOWEY							
-0010	-0015	-0010	-0005	-0.1	-0.1	-0.2	-0.2
LOSTWITHIEL							
+0005	-0010	Dries		-4.1	-4.1	Dries	
PAR							
-0005	-0015	0000	-0010	-0.4	-0.4	-0.4	-0.2

SHELTER
Good, but exposed to winds from S to SW. Gales from these directions can cause heavy swell in the lower hbr and confused seas, especially on the ebb. Entry at any tide in any conditions. Speed limit 6kn. All visitors buoys are White and marked 'FHC VISITORS'.

NAVIGATION
207°/027° from/to Whitehouse Pt lt, Iso WRG 3s. Appr in W sector of Fowey lt ho. W sector of Whitehouse Pt lt leads 027° through hbr ent. 3M E of ent beware Udder Rk marked by unlit SCM buoy. From SW beware Cannis Rk (4ca SE of Gribbin Hd) with SCM buoy, Q (6) + L Fl 15s. Entering hbr, keep well clear of Punch Cross Rks to stbd. Caution: Fowey is a busy commercial clay port. Unmarked chan is navigable up to Golant, but moorings restrict anchoring space. Lerryn (1.6M) and Lostwithiel (3M) are accessible on the tide by shoal draft.

LIGHTS AND MARKS
An unlit RWtr 33m on Gribbin Hd (1.3M WSW of hbr ent) is conspic from all sea directions, as is a white house 3ca E of hbr ent. Lt ho is conspic, L Fl WR 5s 28m 11/9M, R284°-295°, W295°-028°, R028°-054°. Whitehouse Pt Iso WRG 3s 11m 11/8M. G017°-022°. W022°-032°, R032°-037°. Ent is marked by Lamp Rk SHM bn Fl G 5s 7m 2M, vis 088°-205°, and St Catherine's Pt FR 15m 2M, vis 150°-295°.

RADIO TELEPHONE
Call *Fowey* Hbr Radio Ch 12 09 16 (HO). Hbr Patrol (0900-2000LT) Ch 12 16. *Fowey Refueller* Ch 10 16. Water taxi Ch 06. Pilots Ch 09. Tugs Ch 09 12.

FACILITIES
Albert Quay Pontoon L, FW; **Polruan Quay** Slip, P, D, L, FW, C (3 ton); **Royal Fowey YC**, FW, Showers, R, Bar; **Fowey Gallants** SC 832335, Showers, Bar; **Fowey Refueller** (0900-1800LT daily; winter Mon-Fri) VHF Ch 10, 16, D. **Services:** M, FW, Gas, Gaz, CH, ACA.

LOOE

CHARTS
AC 147, 146, 1267; Imray C6; Stanfords 13; OS 201

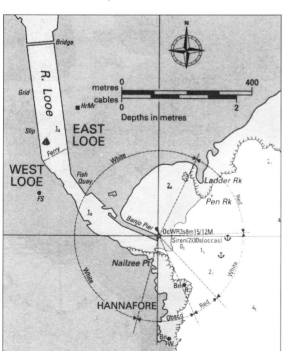

Standard Port PLYMOUTH (→)

Times				Height (metres)			
High Water		Low Water		MHWS	MHWN	MLWN	MLWS
0000	0600	0000	0600	5.5	4.4	2.2	0.8
1200	1800	1200	1800				
Differences LOOE							
-0010	-0010	-0005	-0005	-0.1	-0.2	-0.2	-0.2
WHITSAND BAY							
0000	0000	0000	0000	0.0	+0.1	-0.1	+0.2

SHELTER
Good, but uncomfortable in strong SE winds. anchorage in 2m E of the pier hd; access approx HW ±1¹/₂h. visitors berth, above ferry, is marked in Y on W side of hbr which dries 2.4m to the ent. The W bank has rky outcrops to S of ferry.

NAVIGATION
130°/310° from/to pier hd lt. Ent dangerous in strong SE'lies, when seas break heavily on the bar. From W, beware The Ranneys, rks 2ca SE of Looe Is. Do not attempt the rky passage between Looe Is and mainland except with local knowledge and at HW. From E, beware Longstone Rks extending 1¹/₂ca from shore NE of hbr ent. At sp, ebb tide runs up to 5kn.

LIGHTS AND MARKS
Looe Island (or St George's Is) is conspic (44m), 8ca S of the ent. Mid Main bn (off Hannafore Pt, halfway between pier hd and Looe Is) Q (3) 10s 2M; ECM. At night appr in W sector (267°-313°) of pier hd lt Oc WR 3s 8m 15/12M; vis W013° 207°, R207° 267°, W267° 313°, R313 332; siren (2) 30s, fishing. No lts inside hbr.

RADIO TELEPHONE VHF Ch 16 (occas).

TELEPHONE (Dial code 01503)
Hr Mr 262839; CG 262138; MRSC (01803) 882704; Marinecall 0891 500458; Police 262233; Dr 263195.

FACILITIES
W Looe Quay AB £11.28, Slip, M, P & D (cans), L, FW, ME, El, CH; **E Looe Quay** Access HW ±3, Slip, P & D (cans), L, FW, ME, El, C (2¹/₂ ton); Looe SC 262559, L, R, Bar. **Services:** Sh (Wood), Sh, Gas.

PLYMOUTH (DEVONPORT) Devon

CHARTS
AC *871*, 1902, 1901, *9219*, 1967, 1900, *1267*, 1613; Imray C14; Stanfords 13; OS 201

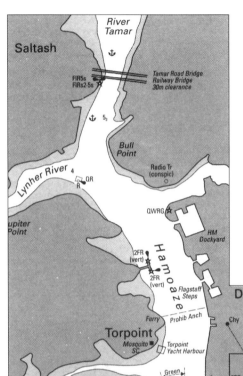

Standard Port PLYMOUTH (→)

Times				Height (metres)			
High Water		Low Water		MHWS	MHWN	MLWN	MLWS
0000	0600	0000	0600	5.5	4.4	2.2	0.8
1200	1800	1200	1800				
Differences BOVISAND PIER							
0000	-0020	0000	-0010	-0.2	-0.1	0.0	+0.1
TURNCHAPEL (Cattewater)							
0000	0000	+0010	-0015	0.0	+0.1	+0.2	+0.1
JUPITER POINT (R. Lynher)							
+0010	+0005	0000	-0005	0.0	0.0	+0.1	0.0
ST GERMANS (R. Lynher)							
0000	0000	+0020	+0020	-0.3	-0.1	0.0	+0.2
SALTASH (R. Tamar)							
0000	+0010	0000	-0005	+0.1	+0.1	+0.1	+0.1
CARGREEN (R. Tamar)							
0000	+0010	+0020	+0020	0.0	0.0	-0.1	0.0
COTEHELE QUAY (R. Tamar)							
0000	+0020	+0045	+0045	-0.9	-0.9	-0.8	-0.4

NOTE: Devonport is a Standard Port; Winds from SE to W increase the flood and retard the ebb; vice versa in winds from the NW to E.

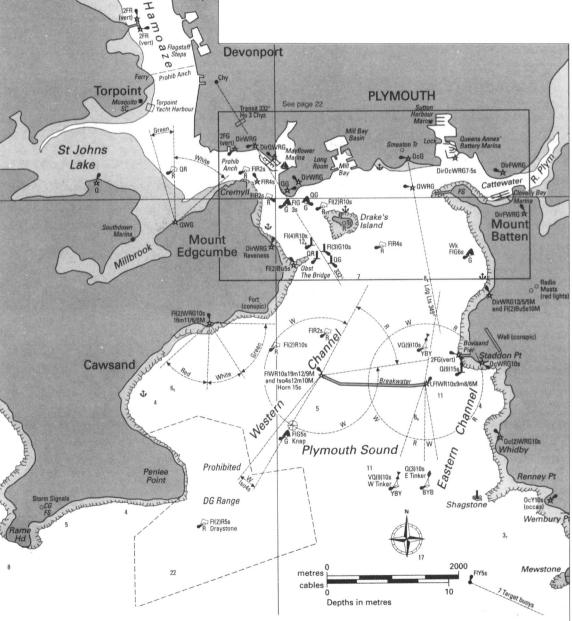

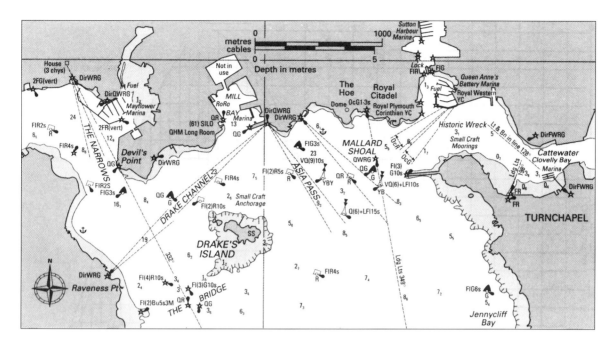

SHELTER

Excellent. Plymouth is a Naval Base, a busy commercial/ferry port principally using Mill Bay Docks, and an active fishing port based mainly on Sutton Harbour which is entered via a lock (see Facilities). There are marinas to E and W of the city centre, as well as in the Cattewater, off Torpoint and in Millbrook Lake. Around the Sound there are anchorages, sheltered according to the wind, in Cawsand Bay, in Barn Pool (below Mt Edgcumbe), N of Drake's Is, below The Hoe and in Jennycliff Bay to the E. Also good shelter W of Cremyll and off the Hamoaze in the R Lynher and in the R Tamar/Tavy above Saltash.

NAVIGATION

213°/033° from/toW bkwtr It. The Sound can be entered via the W or E Chans which are well lit/buoyed with no real hazards. There are no shoal patches with less than 3.7m at MLWS. Yachts need not keep to the deep water chans.

The short cut to the Hamoaze via The Bridge (channel between Drake's Is and Mt Edgcumbe) is lit by 2 PHM and 2 SHM bns; the seaward pair show QR and QG, the inner pair Fl (4) R 10s and Fl (3) G 10s. The QR bn and the Fl (4) R 10s bn both have tide gauges calibrated to show height of tide above CD; charted depth is 2.lm. The E'ly of 3 conspic high-rise blocks brg 331° leads through The Bridge chan. Caution: a charted depth 1.8m is close SW of No 3 SHM bn, Fl (3) G 10s.

Speed limits: l0kn N of The Breakwater, 8kn in Cattewater (where outbound vessels have right of way), 4kn in Sutton Chan and 5kn in Sutton Hbr.

LIGHTS AND MARKS

Bkwtr W hd, Fl WR l0s 19m 12/9M (vis W262°-208°, R208°-262°) and Iso 4s 12m l0M (vis 033°-037°). Bkwtr E hd, L Fl WR l0s 9m 8/6M (R190°-353°, W353°-001°, R001°-018°, W018°-190°). Mallard Shoal ldg Its 349°: Front Q WRG 10/3M (vis G233°-043°, R043°-067°, G067°-087°, W087°-099°, R099°-108°); rear 396m from front (on Hoe) Oc G 1.3s (vis 310°-040°). There are Dir WRG Its, all lit H24 except **,at Whidbey (138.5°), Staddon Pt (044'), Withyhedge (070°), W Hoe bn (315°), Western King (271°), Mill Bay** (048.5°), Raveness (225°), Mount Wise (343°), and Ocean Court** (085°). In fog the following Dir W Its operate: Mallard (front) Fl 5s (vis 232°-110°); West Hoe bn F (vis 313°-317°); Eastern King Fl 5s (vis 259°-062°); Raveness Fl (2)15s (vis 160°- 305°); Mount Wise F (vis 341°-345°); Ocean Court Fl 5s (vis 270°-100°).

Notes: Principal Its in Plymouth Sound show QY if mains power fails. N of The Bkwtr, four large mooring buoys (C, D, E & F) have Fl Y Its.

BYELAWS/NAVAL ACTIVITY

The whole Port is under the jurisdiction of the QHM, but certain areas are locally controlled, i.e. by Cattewater Commissioners and by ABP who operate Mill Bay Docks. Beware frequent movements of naval vessels, which have right of way in the chans. Obey MOD Police orders. Info on Naval activities may be obtained from Naval Ops.

RADIO TELEPHONE

Call: *Long Room Port Control* VHF Ch 08 12 **14** 16 (H24). *Mill Bay Docks* Ch 12 13 14 16 (only during ferry ops). *Sutton Lock*, for lock opening and marina, Ch **12** 16 (H24). *Cattewater Hbr* Ch 14 16 (Mon-Fri, 0900-1700LT). Maytlower, Queen Anne's Battery, Sutton Hbr & Clovelly Bay marinas and Torpoint Yacht Hbr: all Ch **80** M.

FACILITIES

Marinas (W to E)

Torpoint Yacht Hbr (60+20 visitors) £10, access H24, dredged 2m. FW, AC, BY, C, ME, El, Sh, Diver, SM.

Southdown Marina (35 inc visitors) £7.50, access HW±4; AB on pontoon (2m) or on drying quay; FW, AC, D.

Mayflower Marina (300+50 visitors) £18.20 inc AC, P, D, FW, ME, El, Sh, C (2 ton), BH (25 ton), CH, Slip, Gas, Gaz, Divers, SM, BY, YC, V, R, Bar.

Mill Bay Village Marina, VHF Ch M. NO VISITORS. Ent Its = Oc R 4s & Oc G 4s, not on chartlet

Queen Anne's Battery Marina (240+60 visitors) £16.10, AC, P, D, ME, El, Sh, FW, BH (20 ton), C (50 ton), CH, Gas, Gaz, SM, Slip, V, Bar, YC.

Sutton Hbr Marina (310), £15, P, D, FW, AC, El, ME, Sh, CH, C (masts only), Slip. Sutton Hbr is entered via lock (Barbican flood protection scheme), which maintains 3m CD in the marina. Lock (floating fenders) operates H24, free; call *Sutton Lock* VHF Ch 12 16. When tide reaches 3m CD, gates stay open for free-low. Tfc Its (vert): 3 ® = Stop; 3 G = Go; 3 Fl R = Serious hazard, wait.

Clovelly Bay Marina (180+ visitors), £14.48, D, FW, AC, CH, ME, El, Gas, Gaz, V.

Signal	Meaning
Unlit	No restrictions, unless passed on VHF
® ® All Fl ®	Serious Emergency All traffic suspended
® Ⓖ All Oc Ⓖ	Outgoing traffic only may proceed on the recommended track. Crossing traffic to seek approval from Port Control*
Ⓖ Ⓖ All Oc ®	Incoming traffic only may proceed on the recommended track. Crossing traffic to seek approval from Port Control*
Ⓖ Ⓖ All Oc Ⓦ	Vessels may proceed in either direction, but shall give a wide berth to HM Ships using the recommended track

*Call Port Control Ch 13 or 14, but craft <20m LOA may proceed in the contrary direction, with care and not impeding the passage of vessels for which the signal is intended.

DIÉLETTE Manche

CHARTS
AC 3653; SHOM 7133,7158; ECM 528, 1014; Imray C33A; Stanfords 16

TIDES
HW -0430 on Dover (UT); ML 5.2m

Standard Port ST-MALO (→)

Times				Height (metres)			
High Water		Low Water		MHWS	MHWN	MLWN	MLWS
0100	0800	0300	0800	12.2	9.2	4.3	1.6
1300	2000	1500	2000				
Differences FLAMANVILLE							
+0050	+0050	+0025	+0045	-2.7	-1.8	-1.1	-0.5

SHELTER
Good in marina, but do not attempt entry in strong W'lies. Ent dredged to CD, NE part of outer hbr to 2m; access H24 for 1.5m draft if coeff <80. W side of outer hbr dries approx 5m (local moorings). Marina (1.5-2.5m) in SE corner is entered over a sill 4.0m above CD; access about HW±3 for 1.5m draft, waiting pontoon outside.

NAVIGATION
320°/140° from/to W bkwtr lt, 0.40M. Appr is exposed to W'ly winds/swell. Caution: rky reef dries close NE of appr; cross tides at hbr ent. Prohib area from hbr to C de Flamanville extends 5ca offshore.

LIGHTS AND MARKS
Power stn chys (72m) are conspic 1.2M to SW. Dir lt 140°, Iso WRG 4s 12m 10/7M, W tr/G top at hd of West bkwtr, vis G070°-135°, W135°-145° (10°), R145°-180°; on same tr is a lower lt, Fl G 4s 6m 2M. N bkwtr hd, Fl R 4s 8m 5M, W mast/R top. Spur, close SE at ent to new basin, is Fl (2) R 6s 6m 1M.

RADIO TELEPHONE
VHF Ch 09, 0830-2000LT.

FACILITIES
Marina (410) FF124, AC, FW, Fuel, Slip, C (10 ton); **Village**, V, Bar, R. Also facilities at Flamanville (1.3M). Ferry to CI.

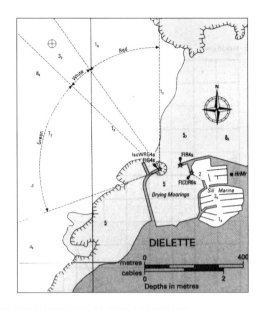

MINOR HARBOUR CLOSE SOUTH OF CAP DE LA HAGUE
GOURY, Manche, AC *1706, 3653;* SHOM 7133 (essential large scale chart), 5636, 7158. HW -0410 on Dover (UT); ML 5.1m. For visitors, appr at slack water nps with no swell and good vis; a fair wx hbr only, dries to flat sand/mud. Cap de la Hague lt, Fl 5s, is 0.5M NW of hbr; La Foraine WCM buoy is 1.1M to the W. Ldg lts: Front QR 4m 7M, on bkwtr hd; rear (110m from front), Q 10m 12M, intens 057°-075°, lead 065° between Charlin to S and Les Grois to N. By day, W patch with R ■ at end of bkwtr on with W pylon of rear ldg lt, 065°. anchor W of the 2 LB slips in 1.7m or dry out on the NE side of the bkwtr. Facilities: R, Bar at Auderville (0.5M).

DAHOUET Côte d'Armor

CHARTS
AC *3674*, 2669; SHOM 7310, 7154, 6966; ECM 536; Imray C33B, C34; Stanfords 16

TIDES
-0520 Dover; ML 6.3; Duration 0550; Zone -0100

Standard Port ST-MALO (→)

Times				Height (metres)			
High Water		Low Water		MHWS	MHWN	MLWN	MLWS
0100	0800	0300	0800	12.2	9.2	4.3	1.6
1300	2000	1500	2000				
Differences DAHOUET							
-0006	-0006	-0020	-0015	-0.9	-0.6	-0.3	-0.3
EROUY							
-0005	0000	-0018	-0012	-0.6	-0.4	-0.1	-0.1
SAINT CAST							
-0002	-0002	-0005	-0005	-0.2	-0.1	-0.1	-0.1

SHELTER
Good, but ent (dries 4m) unsafe in fresh NW winds; a bar may form after strong NW'lies. Outer hbr (FVs) dries 5.5m; access HW±2. Marina min depth 2.5m, accessible over sill 5.5m above CD.

NAVIGATION
Unlit NCM By, 297°/117° from/to La Petite Muette SHM lt tr, 0.8M; appr in W sector until close in. Hbr ent is a narrow break in the cliffs. Pick up 148° transit of 2W bns, leaving these to port and Petite Muette to stbd. The W ent, S of Petite Muette is dangerous. There are rks W and SW of the ent.

LIGHTS AND MARKS
The wide beach at Val André and the W chapel at hbr ent are both conspic; see also Le Légué for other conspic marks in the bay. Appr is marked by G/W lt tr, La Petite Muette, Fl WRG 4s 10m 9/6M, G055°-114°, W114°-146°, R146°-196°. Stone pagoda is seen NE of ent. SHM bn, Fl (2) G 6s, vis 156°-286°, marks the narrow ent abeam the 2 W ldg bns. Sill ent has PHM and SHM perches.

RADIO TELEPHONE
VHF Ch O9 16.

TELEPHONE (Prefix nos with zone code 02)
Hr Mr 96.72.82.65; Météo 36.65.02.22; Customs 96.74.75.32; Aff Mar 96.72.31.42; CROSS 98.89.31.31; Auto 08.36.68.08.22; Brit Consul 99.46.26.64; Police 96.72.22.18.

FACILITIES
Marina (318+20) 96.72.82.85, FF87, FW, AC, BH (10 ton), Slip. C (14 ton); Quay P, D, C (4 ton); **YC du Val- André** 96.72.95.28;

Services:CH, El, ME, Sh. Town, V, R, Bar. Ferry: St. Malo-Portsmouth.

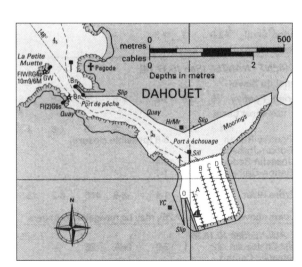

ST QUAY-PORTRIEUX Côte d'Armor

CHARTS
AC 3672, *3674*, 2669, 2668; SHOM 7128, 7154, 6966; ECM 536, 537; Imray C33B, C34; Stanfords 16, 17

TIDES
-0520 Dover; ML 6.3; Duration 0550; Zone -0100

Standard Port ST-MALO (→)

Times				Height (metres)			
High Water		Low Water		MHWS	MHWN	MLWN	MLWS
0100	0800	0300	0800	12.2	9.2	4.3	1.6
1300	2000	1500	2000				
Differences ST QUAY-PORTRIEUX							
-0005	0000	-0020	-0010	-1.0	-0.6	-0.3	-0.2

SHELTER
Excellent in the marina (3.5m). Yachts may also dry out in the Old Hbr. anchorage in the Rade de Pontrieux is good but affected by winds from N to SE.

NAVIGATION
349°/169° from/to NE mole elbow, 2.0M. Portrieux lies inside the Roches de St Quay, the chan between being about ¹/₂M wide. To NE lie the rky lie Harbour and to the E Rochers Déan.
Due N beware the Moulières de Portrieux, unlit ECM bn tr. From E and SE appr via Cafta ECM Q (3) 10s and La Roseliere WCM VQ (9) 10s.

LIGHTS AND MARKS
At night, from the N, White sectors of 4 Dir lts lead safely to the marina in sequence 169°, 130°, 185° (astern), 318° (see chartlet and below):

(1) NE mole elbow, Dir Iso WRG 4s 15/11M, **W159°-179°**, G179°-316°, W316°-**320.5°**, R320.5°-159°

(2) Herflux Dir It, Fl (2) WRG 6s 8/6M, vis G115°-125°, **W125°**-135°, R135°-145°; on Rochers Déan.

(3) Ile Harbour Dir It, Oc (2) WRG 6s 16m 11/8M, vis R011° -133°, G133°-270°, R270°-306°, G306°-358°, W358°-011°.

(4) NE mole elbow, as (1) above, W316°-320.5°.

RADIO TELEPHONE
VHF Ch 09 (0830-1230; 1330-1830LT. H24 in season).

TELEPHONE
(Prefix nos with zone code 02) Marina 96.70.81.30; Hr Mr (Old Hbr) 96.70.95.31; Aff Mar 96.70.42.27; CROSS 98.89.31.31; SNSM 96.70.52.04; Meteo 99.46.10.46; Auto 08.36.68.08.22; Police 96.70.61.24; Dr 96.70.41.31; Brit Consul 99.46.26.64.

FACILITIES
Marina (900+100 visitors) 96.70.81.30, FF130, D, P, FW, BH, AC, C (5 ton);
Old Hbr (500+8 visitors) AB FF60, M, P, D, L, FW, Sh, Slip, C (1.5 ton), ME, El, Sh, CH, R, Bar;

OTHER HARBOURS BETWEEN ST MALO AND DAHOUET

SAINT CAST, Côte d'Armor, AC *3659*, 2669; SHOM 5646, 7155. HW -0515 on Dover (UTI; ML 6.8m; Duration 0550. Good shelter from SW to N winds; Visitors moorings available in 1.8m. Beware Les Bourdinots (dry 2m) with ECM ³/₄M NE of Pte de St Cast, and La Feuilade (IDM bn) and Bec Rond (R bn) off hbr. Mole hd, Iso WG 4s 11m 11/8M; appr in either W sector Hr Mr 02.96.41.88.34; SNSM. Facilities: YC 02.96.41.91.77.
Town CH, El, ME, Sh, ®, Bar, D, P, R, V.
ERQUY, Côte d'Armor, AC 3672, *3674*, 2669; SHOM 7310, 7154. HW-0515 on Dover (UT); ML 6.5m; Duration 0550. Sheltered from E, but exposed to SW/W winds. Hbr dries and is usually full of FVs. Beware Plateau des Portes d'Erquy (dry) about 2M to W. From S, beware rks off Pte de la Houssaye. Mole hd It Oc WRO 12s 11m 11/8M; appr in either W sector. Inner letty hd Fl R 2.5s 10m 3M. Hr Mr 02.96.72.19.32; **Cercle de Na Voile d'Erquy** 02.96.72.32.40; Facilities: **Quay** C (3.5 ton), D, FW, P; Town CH, El, ME, Sh, R, V, Bar.
VAL-ANDRE,
Côte d'Armor, AC *3674*, 2669; SHOM 7310, 7154. HW -0520 on Dover (UT); ML 6.1m; Duration 0550. Tides as Dahouet Small drying hbr exposed to S/SW winds; access HW+3. From the E beware Le Verdelet, and Platier des Trois Têtes from the W. Berth on the quay, ask YC for mooring off Le Piegu or anchor off. Facilities: Hr Mr 02.96.72.83.20, FW, Slip; **YC du Val-André** anchor 02.96.72.21.68; **Town** CH, El, ME, Sh, Bar, R, V.

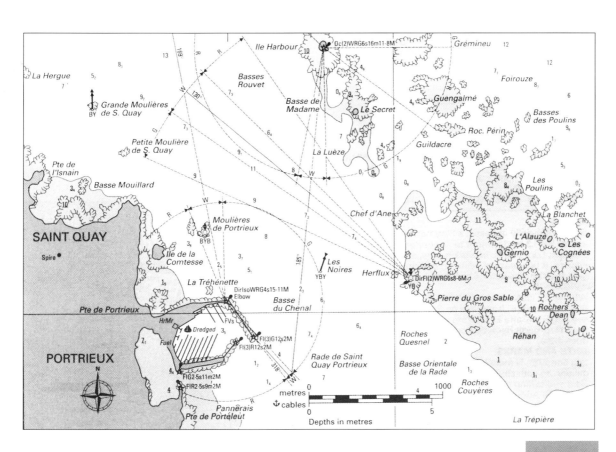

ENGLAND - PLYMOUTH (DEVONPORT)

TIME ZONE (UT)
For Summer Time add ONE hour in non-shaded areas

TIMES AND HEIGHTS OF HIGH AND LOW WATERS

JANUARY

Day	Time	m	Time	m	Time	m	Time	m
1 M	0202	4.5	0821	2.1	1429	4.5	2054	1.9
2 TU	0302	4.7	0925	1.9	1526	4.7	2149	1.7
3 W	0352	4.9	1016	1.6	1615	4.8	2236	1.5
4 TH	0435	5.1	1101	1.4	1656	5.0	2317	1.3
5 F ○	0513	5.2	1141	1.2	1733	5.0	2354	1.2
6 SA	0549	5.3	1217	1.2	1810	5.1		
7 SU	0028	1.2	0626	5.3	1251	1.1	1848	5.1
8 M	0059	1.2	0703	5.3	1321	1.2	1926	5.0
9 TU	0129	1.2	0740	5.2	1351	1.2	2002	5.0
10 W	0159	1.3	0814	5.2	1419	1.3	2034	4.9
11 TH	0228	1.4	0845	5.1	1449	1.4	2104	4.8
12 F	0301	1.5	0918	4.9	1523	1.5	2140	4.7
13 SA	0340	1.7	0959	4.8	1606	1.7	2227	4.6
14 SU	0430	1.9	1052	4.7	1705	1.9	2329	4.5
15 M	0543	2.0	1158	4.6	1831	2.0		
16 TU	0043	4.5	0715	2.0	1316	4.6	1957	1.8
17 W	0206	4.7	0835	1.7	1440	4.8	2110	1.5
18 TH	0321	5.0	0944	1.3	1551	5.0	2214	1.2
19 F	0422	5.3	1045	0.9	1651	5.3	2310	0.8
20 SA ●	0515	5.6	1139	0.6	1744	5.4		
21 SU	0003	0.5	0606	5.8	1231	0.3	1835	5.5
22 M	0052	0.4	0657	5.8	1319	0.2	1926	5.6
23 TU	0138	0.3	0745	5.8	1403	0.2	2012	5.5
24 W	0220	0.3	0830	5.7	1444	0.4	2054	5.4
25 TH	0259	0.7	0911	5.5	1522	0.7	2132	5.2
26 F	0336	1.0	0948	5.2	1559	1.2	2207	4.9
27 SA	0414	1.4	1023	4.9	1638	1.6	2243	4.6
28 SU	0458	1.8	1104	4.5	1726	2.0	2337	4.4
29 M	0555	2.2	1218	4.3	1829	2.2		
30 TU	0107	4.3	0712	2.3	1348	4.2	1956	2.3
31 W	0223	4.4	0848	2.2	1455	4.4	2117	2.0

FEBRUARY

Day	Time	m	Time	m	Time	m	Time	m
1 TH	0322	4.6	0951	1.8	1549	4.6	2211	1.7
2 F	0409	4.9	1039	1.5	1633	4.8	2255	1.4
3 SA	0450	5.1	1120	1.3	1713	5.0	2334	1.2
4 SU ○	0529	5.2	1157	1.1	1752	5.1		
5 M	0009	1.1	0608	5.3	1232	1.0	1831	5.1
6 TU	0042	1.0	0647	5.3	1304	0.9	1910	5.1
7 W	0113	1.0	0725	5.3	1333	0.9	1945	5.1
8 TH	0142	1.0	0758	5.2	1402	1.0	2016	5.0
9 F	0212	1.0	0828	5.2	1431	1.1	2044	5.0
10 SA	0243	1.1	0858	5.1	1503	1.2	2116	4.9
11 SU	0319	1.3	0935	4.9	1541	1.4	2158	4.7
12 M	0403	1.6	1024	4.7	1630	1.7	2255	4.6
13 TU	0505	1.9	1129	4.5	1744	1.9		
14 W	0010	4.5	0637	2.0	1251	4.4	1926	2.0
15 TH	0139	4.6	0813	1.8	1421	4.6	2053	1.7
16 F	0301	4.9	0930	1.4	1538	4.9	2201	1.2
17 SA	0406	5.2	1033	0.9	1638	5.2	2259	0.8
18 SU ●	0501	5.5	1127	0.5	1731	5.4	2349	0.5
19 M	0551	5.7	1216	0.2	1820	5.5		
20 TU	0036	0.2	0639	5.8	1301	0.1	1907	5.6
21 W	0119	0.2	0726	5.8	1343	0.1	1950	5.6
22 TH	0159	0.3	0808	5.7	1419	0.3	2027	5.4
23 F	0235	0.5	0844	5.5	1455	0.7	2057	5.2
24 SA	0308	0.9	0912	5.2	1527	1.1	2121	5.0
25 SU	0341	1.3	0936	4.8	1600	1.5	2149	4.7
26 M	0418	1.7	1008	4.5	1630	1.7	2231	4.4
27 TU	0507	2.1	1059	4.2	1737	2.3	2336	4.2
28 W	0617	2.4	1241	4.0	1853	2.4		
29 TH	0133	4.2	0745	2.3	1421	4.2	2027	2.2

MARCH

Day	Time	m	Time	m	Time	m	Time	m
1 F	0248	4.4	0918	2.0	1521	4.4	2140	1.9
2 SA	0341	4.7	1011	1.6	1608	4.7	2227	1.5
3 SU	0425	5.0	1052	1.3	1650	4.9	2307	1.2
4 M	0506	5.2	1130	1.0	1730	5.1	2344	1.0
5 TU ○	0546	5.3	1206	0.9	1810	5.2		
6 W	0019	0.8	0625	5.3	1240	0.8	1848	5.2
7 TH	0052	0.8	0703	5.3	1312	0.7	1924	5.2
8 F	0123	0.8	0738	5.3	1342	0.8	1955	5.2
9 SA	0154	0.8	0810	5.2	1413	0.9	2024	5.1
10 SU	0227	0.9	0843	5.1	1445	1.0	2057	5.0
11 M	0303	1.1	0920	4.9	1522	1.3	2139	4.8
12 TU	0347	1.4	1008	4.7	1612	1.6	2234	4.6
13 W	0447	1.8	1113	4.5	1722	1.9	2349	4.5
14 TH	0616	1.9	1238	4.4	1906	2.0		
15 F	0121	4.5	0758	1.8	1410	4.5	2039	1.7
16 SA	0245	4.8	0917	1.4	1526	4.8	2148	1.3
17 SU	0350	5.2	1018	0.9	1624	5.1	2243	0.8
18 M	0443	5.5	1109	0.5	1714	5.4	2331	0.5
19 TU ●	0532	5.6	1156	0.3	1800	5.5		
20 W	0016	0.3	0618	5.7	1239	0.1	1842	5.6
21 TH	0057	0.2	0702	5.7	1319	0.2	1922	5.5
22 F	0135	0.3	0741	5.6	1355	0.4	1955	5.4
23 SA	0209	0.5	0813	5.4	1427	0.7	2020	5.2
24 SU	0241	0.9	0837	5.1	1457	1.1	2043	5.0
25 M	0311	1.3	0901	4.8	1527	1.5	2113	4.8
26 TU	0344	1.7	0935	4.5	1602	1.9	2153	4.5
27 W	0429	2.1	1022	4.2	1655	2.3	2249	4.3
28 TH	0536	2.3	1134	4.0	1810	2.4		
29 F	0016	4.2	0654	2.3	1337	4.1	1928	2.3
30 SA	0204	4.3	0816	2.1	1446	4.3	2047	2.0
31 SU	0305	4.6	0924	1.7	1537	4.6	2146	1.6

APRIL

Day	Time	m	Time	m	Time	m	Time	m
1 M	0354	4.9	1013	1.3	1621	4.9	2231	1.3
2 TU	0437	5.1	1054	1.1	1703	5.1	2312	1.0
3 W	0519	5.3	1134	0.8	1743	5.2	2351	0.8
4 TH ○	0559	5.3	1211	0.7	1822	5.3		
5 F	0028	0.7	0638	5.4	1248	0.6	1858	5.3
6 SA	0104	0.6	0716	5.4	1323	0.7	1933	5.3
7 SU	0139	0.7	0753	5.3	1357	0.8	2008	5.3
8 M	0215	0.8	0831	5.2	1434	1.0	2045	5.2
9 TU	0254	1.0	0912	5.0	1514	1.3	2128	5.0
10 W	0341	1.3	1002	4.7	1605	1.6	2223	4.8
11 TH	0441	1.6	1107	4.5	1715	1.9	2337	4.6
12 F	0606	1.8	1231	4.4	1851	2.0		
13 SA	0107	4.6	0741	1.7	1357	4.5	2020	1.7
14 SU	0225	4.8	0857	1.4	1507	4.8	2127	1.3
15 M	0329	5.1	0956	1.0	1603	5.1	2222	0.9
16 TU	0422	5.3	1047	0.6	1651	5.3	2309	0.6
17 W ●	0509	5.5	1132	0.4	1735	5.4	2353	0.4
18 TH	0554	5.5	1214	0.4	1816	5.5		
19 F	0033	0.4	0635	5.5	1253	0.5	1852	5.4
20 SA	0110	0.5	0712	5.4	1328	0.6	1923	5.4
21 SU	0144	0.7	0742	5.2	1400	0.9	1948	5.2
22 M	0215	1.0	0807	5.0	1430	1.2	2015	5.1
23 TU	0246	1.3	0836	4.8	1459	1.5	2048	4.9
24 W	0317	1.6	0912	4.6	1531	1.9	2127	4.7
25 TH	0357	1.9	0957	4.3	1617	2.1	2216	4.4
26 F	0458	2.2	1058	4.1	1728	2.3	2323	4.3
27 SA	0612	2.2	1228	4.1	1843	2.3		
28 SU	0054	4.3	0722	2.1	1356	4.3	1951	2.1
29 M	0215	4.5	0826	1.8	1456	4.6	2054	1.7
30 TU	0313	4.8	0924	1.4	1545	4.8	2148	1.4

Chart Datum: 3·22 metres below Ordnance Datum (Newlyn)

TIME ZONE –0100
(French Standard Time)
Subtract 1 hour for UT

For French Summer Time add
ONE hour in non-shaded areas

FRANCE - ST. MALO

TIMES AND HEIGHTS OF HIGH AND LOW WATERS

MAY

Day	Time	m	Day	Time	m
1 W	0527 / 1219 / 1753	10.7 / 2.6 / 11.1	**16** TH	0048 / 0612 / 1308 / 1830	2.2 / 11.4 / 2.0 / 11.6
2 TH	0036 / 0609 / 1304 / 1832	2.4 / 11.3 / 2.1 / 11.7	**17** F ●	0131 / 0654 / 1347 / 1907	2.0 / 11.6 / 1.9 / 11.8
3 F O	0122 / 0650 / 1348 / 1911	1.8 / 11.8 / 1.6 / 12.1	**18** SA	0209 / 0732 / 1422 / 1942	1.9 / 11.6 / 1.8 / 11.8
4 SA	0206 / 0730 / 1429 / 1949	1.4 / 12.1 / 1.3 / 12.4	**19** SU	0243 / 0806 / 1454 / 2014	1.8 / 11.6 / 1.9 / 11.7
5 SU	0249 / 0810 / 1508 / 2027	1.1 / 12.3 / 1.3 / 12.4	**20** M	0315 / 0839 / 1525 / 2045	1.9 / 11.4 / 2.1 / 11.5
6 M	0329 / 0851 / 1546 / 2108	1.1 / 12.2 / 1.5 / 12.2	**21** TU	0346 / 0911 / 1556 / 2116	2.2 / 11.0 / 2.5 / 11.1
7 TU	0409 / 0934 / 1625 / 2151	1.4 / 11.8 / 1.9 / 11.8	**22** W	0416 / 0943 / 1625 / 2150	2.7 / 10.6 / 3.0 / 10.6
8 W	0451 / 1020 / 1708 / 2238	1.8 / 11.2 / 2.5 / 11.1	**23** TH	0446 / 1019 / 1658 / 2227	3.2 / 10.0 / 3.6 / 10.1
9 TH	0538 / 1113 / 1758 / 2336	2.5 / 10.5 / 3.1 / 10.4	**24** F	0521 / 1100 / 1738 / 2312	3.7 / 9.5 / 4.1 / 9.5
10 F	0637 / 1218 / 1903	3.1 / 9.9 / 3.6	**25** SA	0606 / 1156 / 1832	4.1 / 9.0 / 4.5

JUNE

Day	Time	m	Day	Time	m
1 SA O	0051 / 0622 / 1320 / 1844	1.9 / 11.6 / 1.7 / 12.1	**16** SU ●	0143 / 0711 / 1357 / 1920	2.3 / 11.1 / 2.3 / 11.5
2 SU	0143 / 0709 / 1408 / 1929	1.4 / 12.0 / 1.4 / 12.4	**17** M	0220 / 0747 / 1432 / 1954	2.2 / 11.2 / 2.2 / 11.5
3 M	0233 / 0756 / 1454 / 2014	1.1 / 12.3 / 1.2 / 12.6	**18** TU	0255 / 0821 / 1506 / 2027	2.1 / 11.2 / 2.3 / 11.5
4 TU	0320 / 0843 / 1538 / 2059	1.0 / 12.3 / 1.3 / 12.5	**19** W	0328 / 0854 / 1539 / 2059	2.2 / 11.0 / 2.4 / 11.3
5 W	0405 / 0930 / 1622 / 2146	1.1 / 12.1 / 1.6 / 12.1	**20** TH	0359 / 0927 / 1609 / 2131	2.5 / 10.8 / 2.7 / 11.0
6 TH	0451 / 1018 / 1707 / 2234	1.5 / 11.6 / 2.1 / 11.6	**21** F	0430 / 1001 / 1640 / 2206	2.8 / 10.5 / 3.1 / 10.6
7 F	0539 / 1108 / 1755 / 2327	2.0 / 11.0 / 2.7 / 10.9	**22** SA	0501 / 1037 / 1715 / 2244	3.2 / 10.0 / 3.5 / 10.1
8 SA	0631 / 1203 / 1852	2.6 / 10.4 / 3.3	**23** SU	0538 / 1119 / 1756 / 2328	3.6 / 9.6 / 3.9 / 9.6
9 SU	0027 / 0731 / 1305 / 1958	10.3 / 3.2 / 9.9 / 3.7	**24** M	0622 / 1211 / 1847	4.0 / 9.2 / 4.2
10 M	0136 / 0837 / 1416 / 2111	9.9 / 3.4 / 9.7 / 3.8	**25** TU	0024 / 0719 / 1316 / 1950	9.2 / 4.2 / 9.0 / 4.3

JULY

Day	Time	m	Day	Time	m
1 M O	0124 / 0653 / 1352 / 1915	1.5 / 12.0 / 1.4 / 12.5	**16** TU	0202 / 0730 / 1415 / 1937	2.4 / 11.1 / 2.4 / 11.5
2 TU	0220 / 0745 / 1444 / 2004	1.1 / 12.4 / 1.2 / 12.8	**17** W	0238 / 0804 / 1449 / 2010	2.2 / 11.2 / 2.3 / 11.6
3 W	0312 / 0835 / 1532 / 2051	0.8 / 12.6 / 1.1 / 12.9	**18** TH	0311 / 0837 / 1521 / 2041	2.2 / 11.2 / 2.3 / 11.5
4 TH	0401 / 0922 / 1617 / 2138	0.8 / 12.5 / 1.3 / 12.6	**19** F	0342 / 0908 / 1551 / 2112	2.3 / 11.1 / 2.4 / 11.4
5 F	0446 / 1008 / 1701 / 2223	1.1 / 12.1 / 1.7 / 12.1	**20** SA	0411 / 0939 / 1621 / 2143	2.5 / 10.9 / 2.6 / 11.0
6 SA	0530 / 1052 / 1743 / 2309	1.7 / 11.5 / 2.4 / 11.3	**21** SU	0440 / 1011 / 1652 / 2216	2.8 / 10.6 / 3.0 / 10.6
7 SU	0614 / 1138 / 1829 / 2358	2.4 / 10.8 / 3.1 / 10.5	**22** M	0511 / 1045 / 1726 / 2251	3.2 / 10.1 / 3.4 / 10.1
8 M	0700 / 1228 / 1921	3.2 / 10.1 / 3.8	**23** TU	0547 / 1124 / 1808 / 2335	3.6 / 9.7 / 3.8 / 9.6
9 TU	0055 / 0755 / 1329 / 2025	9.8 / 3.8 / 9.6 / 4.2	**24** W	0633 / 1215 / 1901	4.0 / 9.3 / 4.2
10 W	0206 / 0900 / 1443 / 2140	9.4 / 4.1 / 9.4 / 4.2	**25** TH	0037 / 0735 / 1329 / 2012	9.2 / 4.2 / 9.2 / 4.2

AUGUST

Day	Time	m	Day	Time	m
1 TH	0302 / 0823 / 1522 / 2040	0.6 / 12.9 / 0.8 / 13.2	**16** F	0251 / 0815 / 1501 / 2020	2.1 / 11.5 / 2.1 / 11.8
2 F	0350 / 0908 / 1606 / 2123	0.5 / 12.9 / 0.9 / 13.0	**17** SA	0320 / 0845 / 1531 / 2050	2.1 / 11.5 / 2.1 / 11.7
3 SA	0432 / 0949 / 1646 / 2204	0.9 / 12.5 / 1.4 / 12.4	**18** SU	0349 / 0914 / 1600 / 2119	2.1 / 11.3 / 2.2 / 11.5
4 SU	0511 / 1029 / 1722 / 2244	1.5 / 11.8 / 2.2 / 11.5	**19** M	0417 / 0944 / 1630 / 2149	2.4 / 11.1 / 2.5 / 11.0
5 M	0546 / 1106 / 1758 / 2324	2.4 / 11.0 / 3.1 / 10.6	**20** TU	0446 / 1014 / 1701 / 2221	2.8 / 10.6 / 3.0 / 10.5
6 TU	0622 / 1147 / 1837	3.3 / 10.1 / 3.9	**21** W	0519 / 1048 / 1738 / 2300	3.3 / 10.1 / 3.5 / 9.9
7 W	0010 / 0706 / 1238 / 1933	9.6 / 4.1 / 9.4 / 4.6	**22** TH	0600 / 1133 / 1826 / 2357	3.8 / 9.5 / 4.0 / 9.3
8 TH	0115 / 0808 / 1353 / 2053	9.0 / 4.6 / 8.9 / 4.8	**23** F	0657 / 1244 / 1935	4.2 / 9.2 / 4.3
9 F	0249 / 0929 / 1524 / 2217	8.8 / 4.6 / 9.1 / 4.4	**24** SA	0127 / 0822 / 1422 / 2110	9.1 / 4.3 / 9.3 / 4.0
10 SA	0410 / 1045 / 1633 / 2324	9.2 / 4.2 / 9.7 / 3.8	**25** SU	0310 / 0958 / 1550 / 2240	9.5 / 3.8 / 10.0 / 3.3

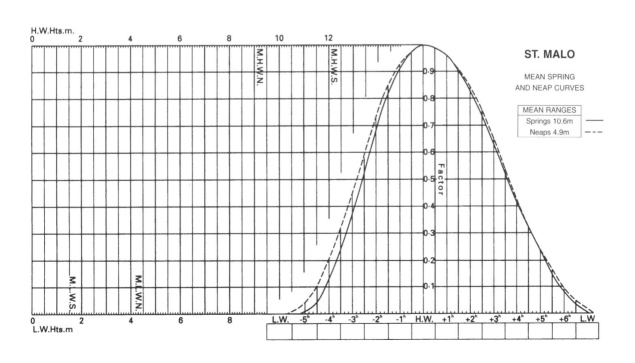

ST. MALO

MEAN SPRING
AND NEAP CURVES

MEAN RANGES	
Springs 10.6m	——
Neaps 4.9m	- - -

TIDAL STREAM CHARTS

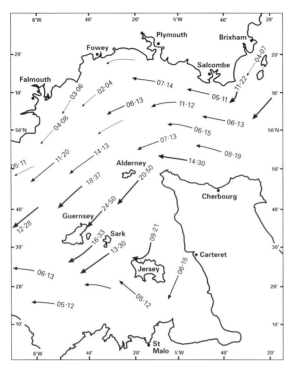

**5 hours before HW Plymouth
(2 hours after HW Dover)**

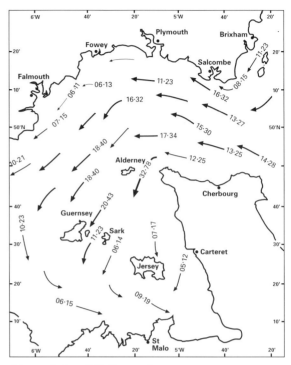

**4 hours before HW Plymouth
(3 hours after HW Dover)**

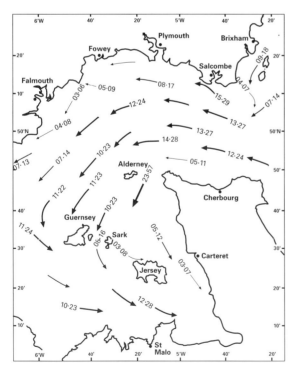

**3 hours before HW Plymouth
(4 hours after HW Dover)**

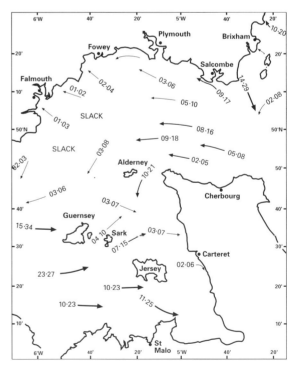

**2 hours before HW Plymouth
(5 hours after HW Dover)**

TIDAL STREAM CHARTS

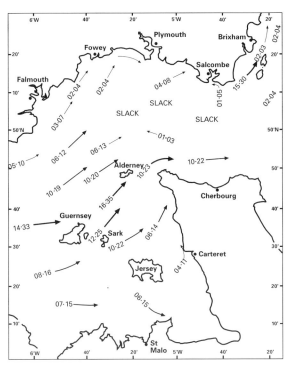

1 hour before HW Plymouth
(6 hours after HW Dover)

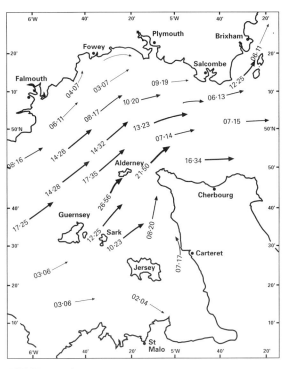

HW Plymouth
(5 hours before HW Dover)

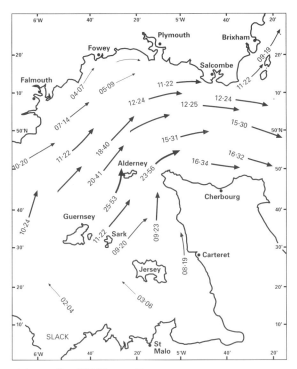

1 hour after HW Plymouth
(4 hours before HW Dover)

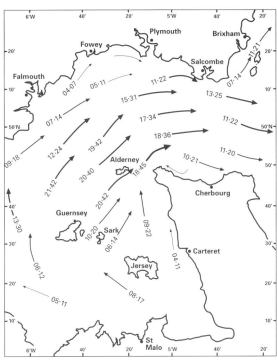

2 hours after HW Plymouth
(3 hours before HW Dover)

85

TIDAL STREAM CHARTS

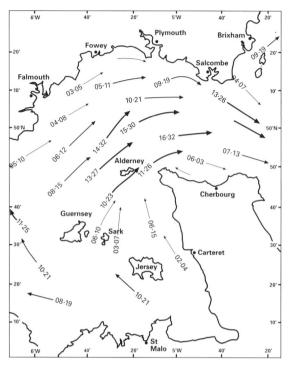

3 hours after HW Plymouth
(2 hours before HW Dover)

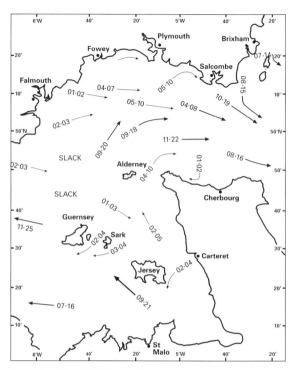

4 hours after HW Plymouth
(1 hour before HW Dover)

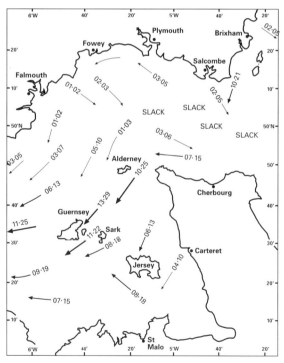

5 hours after HW Plymouth
(HW Dover)

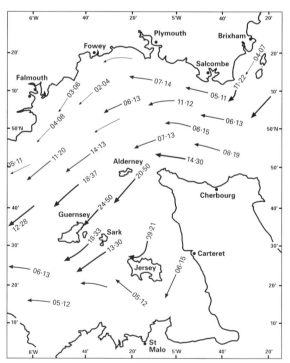

6 hours after HW Plymouth
(1 hour after HW Dover)

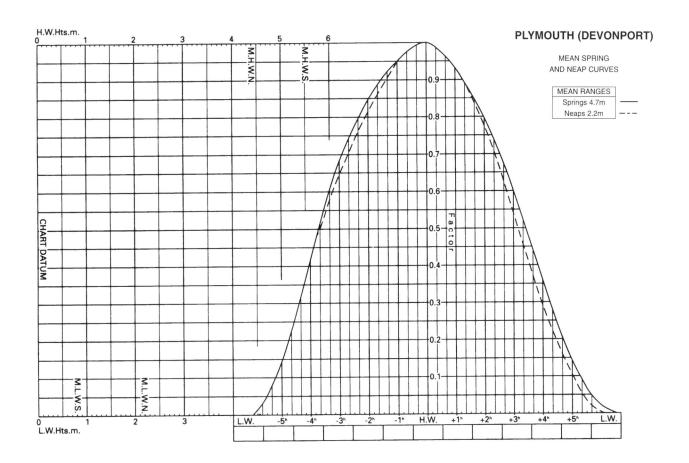

PLYMOUTH (DEVONPORT)

MEAN SPRING
AND NEAP CURVES

MEAN RANGES	
Springs 4.7m	———
Neaps 2.2m	- - -

COMPASS DEVIATION TABLE

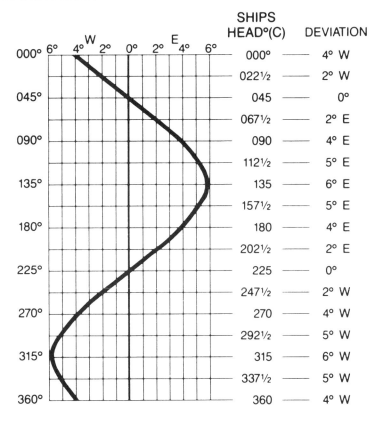

SHIPS HEAD°(C)	DEVIATION
000°	4° W
022½	2° W
045	0°
067½	2° E
090	4° E
112½	5° E
135	6° E
157½	5° E
180	4° E
202½	2° E
225	0°
247½	2° W
270	4° W
292½	5° W
315	6° W
337½	5° W
360	4° W

COMPUTATION OF RATES

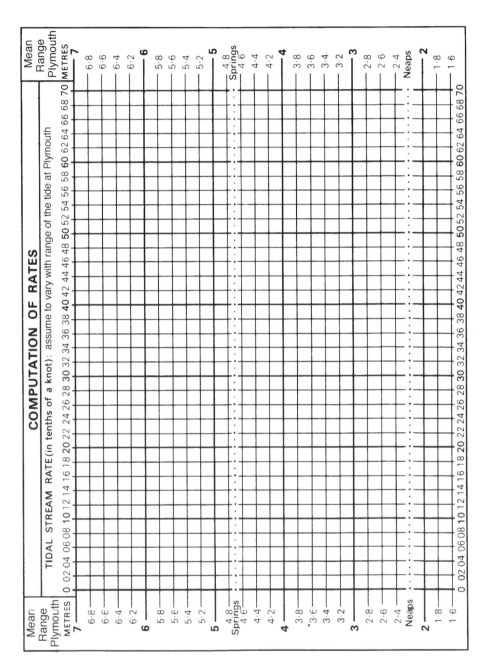

COMPUTATION OF RATES - USE OF DIAGRAM

Example to predict the rate of tidal stream at 0756 BST on Friday 7 June in the Alderney Race using the data from the tidal stream atlas.
From Plymouth tide table (page 24).

LW 0440 (BST) 0.9m ⎫
                    ⎬ **Range 4.1m**
HW 1056 (BST) 5.0m ⎭

From the tidal stream atlas (page 6), 0756 (BST) = 3 hours before HW Plymouth. The rates in the Alderney Race would be **2.3kn** (neaps) **5.7kn** (springs).

Using the computation of rates table: -
(1) Where the dotted neaps line intersects **2.3kn** make a small circle around the dot.
(2) Where the dotted springs line intersects **5.7kn** make a small circle around the dot.
(3) Join these marks with a straight line.
(4) Draw a horizontal line from **4.1m** (the morning range) until it intersects the line drawn in step 3.
(5) From this intersection draw a vertical line, up or down, and note the tidal stream rate, in this example **4.9kn.**